Leckie
the education publisher
for Scotland

Higher
GRAPHIC COMMUNICATION

For SQA 2019 and beyond

Course Notes

Barry Forbes

Table of contents

The contents of this book are guided by the Higher Graphic Communication Course Assessment Specification. You should be aware of the content of this document as it will help you pass the subject.

CONTENTS

Gaining your qualification

To be awarded a Higher Graphic Communication qualification you must complete an assignment that is set annually and an exam. You will gain the knowledge and skills required to complete the assignment and pass the exam through your coursework. All of the skills and knowledge you need to pass the course are described within the Higher Graphic Communication Course Specification. This is a very important document. You should refer to it throughout the course to evaluate your knowledge against what you need to know.

Covering the content of the course specification

Different methods can be used to cover the content included in the course specification. A number of examples of projects that you could complete in order to cover the course specification at Higher Graphic Communication are included in this book. These projects show how all the course content can be met naturally through coursework projects set in real-life contexts to keep learning relevant.

The course assignment

You will complete an assessment project given to you by your assessor and set annually by the SQA. The sports shaker bottle project in this book is not an SQA set assignment – it is here to show how you could go about completing an assignment in order to gain a good mark.

The exam

This book covers everything you need to know to pass the exam.

The exam will assess your understanding of the subject. You will need to study and prepare carefully in order to perform at your best level. Try not to worry about the exam. Preparation is the key to doing well. The content of the exam is predictable as it is listed in the course specification, which can be found on the Higher Graphic Communication page of the SQA website. Use the practice papers and SQA past papers, available free of charge from the SQA website, to test your understanding and prepare for it.

The course assignment and exam are covered in greater detail towards the end of this book.

The Graphic Communication course

The new Graphic Communication courses have been designed to be relevant to the demands of modern industry. The types of graphics you will learn about fall into three categories:

1. Preliminary
2. Production
3. Promotional

These names will not be new to you. You will be familiar with them from the work you completed during National 5. At Higher level, you will be required to produce drawings of a higher quality and complexity, using more advanced commands and more in-depth research.

You will develop your ability to produce preliminary graphics when tackling a graphic brief. This includes using a range of techniques to produce high-quality manual graphics.

At the centre of production graphics is 3D modelling. You will use 3D modelling software throughout your studies in this course. This provides you with an industry standard education, so you are excellently prepared for the world of work or university. You will learn many facets of 3D modelling, including different modelling commands and edits, assembly methods and rendering techniques.

You will plan, develop and create a variety of promotional graphics using the design elements and principles of desktop publishing (DTP). You will also develop your knowledge and ability to apply DTP commands in order to produce high-quality presentations.

Course assessment

Once you have developed your skills and knowledge in these areas, you will begin the course assessment. This consists of an assignment (which you will complete in class) and an exam (which you will sit as part of the SQA diet in May).

You will complete the assignment project under a high degree of supervision and control. This means that you are not permitted to access the Internet or other resources or to receive any help from anyone during the project. Your assignment is then sent away to the SQA to be marked externally. The assignment is marked out of 50.

The exam is marked out of 90 and is also marked externally by the SQA marking teams.

Your final award for the course is decided by adding your marks for the assignment and exam together, and calculating a percentage from this.

While the grade boundaries can move by one or two marks each year from the notional values given below, this is a general guide:

Grade A: 70% and above
Grade B: 60–69%
Grade C: 50–59%
Grade D: 40–49%

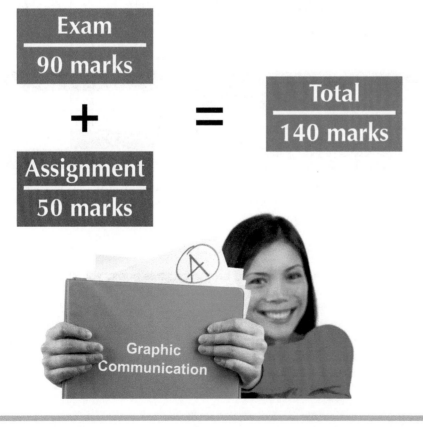

Exam
90 marks

+

Assignment
50 marks

=

Total
140 marks

This book will provide you with all the information you need in order to pass Higher Graphic Communication. It covers all the necessary coursework and contains tips for your assignment and exam.

It does not use official SQA tasks, but the included examples show how you can plan your work to ensure success within Higher Graphic Communication.

There are a number of topics that you must know about. The contents page of this book lists these topics. They can also be found in the course specification. This is an important document for the Higher Graphic Communication course and one that your assessor will be familiar with and will provide you with. You can access this at any time from the SQA website.

This book includes 'Assignment Advice' and 'Exam Tip' boxes throughout. Your final grade for the course is calculated from your marks for the assignment and exam. These boxes identify important points to help you achieve the best marks possible in both.

GO! Assignment Advice

These boxes contain advice to help you complete your assignment.

GO! Exam Tip

These boxes contain hints and tips that will help prepare you for your exam.

Course outline

There are many ways of planning your learning throughout the year. It is a good idea to plan your time so you can structure your learning and ensure you cover all the relevant parts of the course. Your learning plan could look like the one below.

Unit of work	June	August	September	October	November	December	January	February	March	April
Scented project	■	■								
Magazine layout		■	■							
Dimensioning and tolerances			■	■						
Carabiner clip project				■	■					
Sports shaker bottle project					■	■				
Drawing board unit – tangency and interpenetration						■	■			
Knowledge and understanding	■	■	■							
Exam question practice		■	■	■	■	■	■	■	■	■
Prelim revision							■	■		
Assignment preparation								■		
Assignment								■	■	
Exam revision										■

Coursework

You should use the question booklet that accompanies this book as you are working through the content to help you remember the key points you will need to know. You can find the booklet here: www.collins.co.uk/pages/Scottish-curriculum-free-resources.

The key areas of coursework will almost certainly be covered through project work which will help you to learn about preliminary, production and promotional styles of graphics. You will learn the purpose of these graphics and how to produce them. It is likely your teacher will explore areas such as design elements and principles or how to use 3D CAD and then introduce a project for you to complete using this newly learned knowledge.

The projects in this book can also be accessed at www.collins.co.uk/pages/Scottish-curriculum-free-resources. These can be downloaded free of charge for you to work through independently or for your teacher to use during your course. You will develop all of the knowledge and skills required for the course while working through these projects.

Preparing for your assignment

In addition to working through the projects in this book, you should complete some past assignments. Your teacher will be able to provide the electronic files required to do this. You should time yourself when completing these assignments to ensure that you get an accurate idea of how you will be able to perform in the actual assignment. Remember to try and stick to the rules that will guide the real assignment when you are completing practice assignments. In particular, you should only use the files given to you, not look at your notes for assistance and not use the Internet for help.

Preparing for your exam

Make sure you spend some time practising exam-style questions. This should be part of your weekly revision for the course from the outset. You can print the SQA past papers, which are available free of charge from the SQA website. Alternatively, your teacher may choose to use the digital versions of the exam papers and issue them as assignments using a digital classroom.

Why is this subject useful for you?

One of the world's emerging technologies is 3D printing. In order to be able to 3D print anything, someone has to create a 3D CAD model of the product. The only limitation on what can be 3D printed is the size of the 3D printer. If the printer is large enough, then buildings can be 3D printed. Prosthetic limbs for children are increasingly being 3D printed because it is quicker and cheaper and because different sizes of prosthetics can easily be produced depending on the size and age of a child.

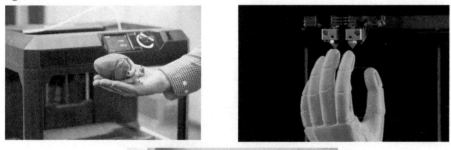

Sketching and rendering is a skill that you can use in a range of industries where a quick idea is required to gauge scale, size, proportion, colour and the material required for a project. Whether that be product based, engineering solutions or building designs, these skills are transferable to a wide range of applications.

The use of augmented reality is growing worldwide within a variety of contexts. You will be able to use the knowledge and skills you develop throughout this course to work in this field.

The DTP skills that you develop can be used in a range of areas from web design to developing a range of promotional materials, including t-shirts, mugs, marketing brochures and electronic advertisements.

Chapter 1

Types of Graphic

You will learn

- Types of graphic
- Preliminary graphics
- Types of sketches
- Production graphics
- Promotional graphics

Types of graphic

There are three main types of graphic that are produced during the process of developing new products or engineering solutions. These are:

1. Preliminary graphics

2. Production graphics

3. Promotional graphics

This section provides a brief overview of why and how the different types of graphics are created. The techniques mentioned are covered in more detail later in the book.

Preliminary graphics

Preliminary graphics are initial hand-drawn sketches. These can be produced using traditional methods, such as colour pencils or spirit marker pens.

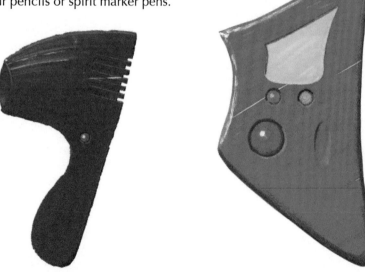

Why are they produced?

Preliminary graphics are used to give the client an idea of what the product will look like. They also help the design engineers to develop new ideas quickly, before taking the more effective solutions forward to develop.

Manual techniques

Using marker pens and colour pencils requires a great deal of skill. Graphic designers use tried and trusted methods to produce 2D images that appear to be 3D.

Highlights and lowlights

Highlights can be used to make it look like light is reflecting from a surface. A white line can be used to show light falling on sharp edges. This effect can be created using white pencils, correction pens or by leaving a gap when marker rendering on white paper.

Lowlights are created using black pencils and show areas of low light and shadows on the sketch.

Tone

Where more layers of a colour are applied, this is called tone. Tonal scale is clearly shown in the graphic below. It is used to show the gradual change in light in a sketch. It can be used in both pencil and marker pen sketches.

Texture

A graphic designer can indicate different textures where they are proposed to be used on a product.

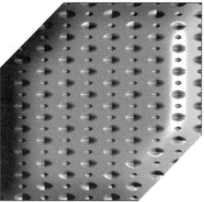

Material

Different materials should be shown to demonstrate where they will be used or combined in an engineering solution. This can be done using a variety of techniques.

Electronic methods of producing preliminary graphics

Tablets with sketching apps, such as Autodesk Sketchbook or Adobe Photoshop Sketch, can be used with a stylus pen to create electronic preliminary sketches. These allow the user to input hand-drawn sketches directly into the computer, without having to master the use of a mouse for drawing. This can be used to apply high-quality rendering using computer software. Rendering is the process of showing shape, form, texture and light on an object to make it look realistic. Rendering can be completed using both manual and computer methods – manual during the preliminary stages and computer generated during the promotional stages.

Because these electronic methods allow initial sketches to be produced immediately onto a computer, ideas can be shared quickly through email with anyone in the world. This allows multinational companies to develop and share initial sketches for products from different countries around the world.

Types of sketches

You should be able to sketch using both orthographic and pictorial methods.

Orthographic sketching

When you sketch components orthographically, you have to follow the same drawing conventions you would if using a drawing board. Both the plan and end elevation must be projected from the elevation. The depths of the end elevation must be projected from the plan.

Orthographic sketches and drawings must project from each other. In other words, the heights, widths and depths must follow each other exactly in each of the views. You can see how these three views of the sharpener are drawn directly above and to the side of one another, with all of the details within the views lining up. This is a vital part of third-angle projection.

It is good practice to sketch the third-angle projection symbol on the sheet to let people know which projection method is being used.

These sketches must also be produced to good proportions. Proportions are important to graphically convey shape and size to a client. Think of line lengths as fractions. As an example, if one line should be half as long as another, then you must show it as this.

Any dimensions or sectional views must follow British Standard conventions.

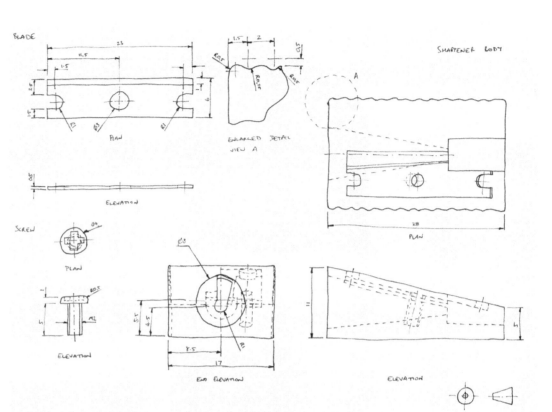
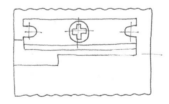

Once the initial sketches have been used to give an indication of the shape and form of a product, you need to produce orthographic sketches of it. These must be dimensioned to show sufficient detail to allow 3D models of the product to be developed to prepare for manufacture.

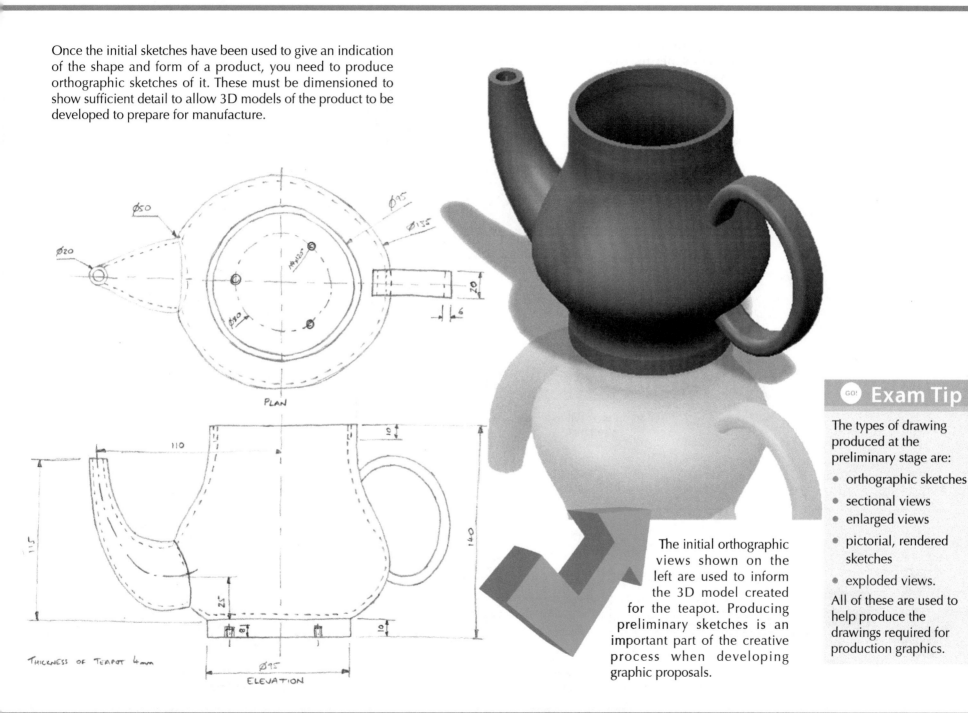

PLAN

ELEVATION

THICKNESS OF TEAPOT 4mm

GO! Exam Tip

The types of drawing produced at the preliminary stage are:

- orthographic sketches
- sectional views
- enlarged views
- pictorial, rendered sketches
- exploded views.

All of these are used to help produce the drawings required for production graphics.

The initial orthographic views shown on the left are used to inform the 3D model created for the teapot. Producing preliminary sketches is an important part of the creative process when developing graphic proposals.

Pictorial sketching

You should learn a range of pictorial sketching techniques, including isometric, one-point perspective and two-point perspective methods. You should also ensure that you show technical detail, including how different components of a product fit together using sectional views and/or exploded views where appropriate. These do not have to show the product in its entirety – technical detail can often be shown as an enlarged view to show the relevant parts more clearly.

Rendered pictorial assembly sketches.

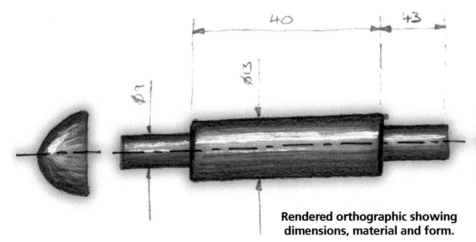

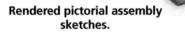

Rendered orthographic showing dimensions, material and form.

Exploded pictorial sketches showing material and form.

Production graphics

Production graphics are vital for a product or engineering component to be manufactured. They are fully dimensioned and contain technical detail, such as sectional views, enlarged views, component views, exploded views and pictorial views.

Production drawings are often produced from a 3D model created in software. This allows the drawings to be created very quickly. They will also be updated automatically if any changes are made to the 3D model.

It tends to be the orthographic views of the components of an object that have dimensions added to them. This is so that the drawings are clear to understand. Assembly orthographics and pictorial views may include some dimensions, but only those that are vital to understanding how the different parts of an object fit together.

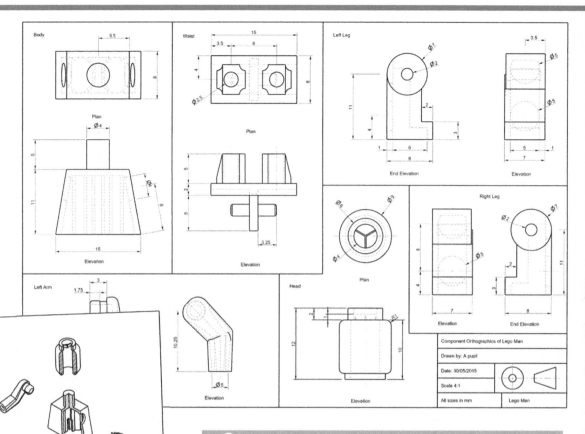

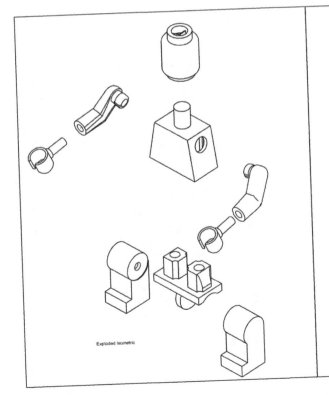

GO! Exam Tip

The types of drawings produced at the production stage are:

- orthographic views
- sectional views, including stepped sections
- enlarged views
- isometric views
- exploded isometric views.

GO! Assignment Advice

You have to show dimensioned component orthographics, enlarged views, stepped sections, plus assembled and exploded isometric views in your assignment.

Promotional graphics

Promotional graphics can take a number of different forms:

- magazine articles
- roller banners
- folding leaflets
- table stands
- posters
- web pages
- business cards
- tablet or app display rendered environments.

Promotional graphics are used to promote or advertise a product. They should be attractive to look at and most often follow layout rules known as 'design elements and principles'. These are explained later in this book.

Promotional graphics tend to be produced using DTP software on computers. It is common for there to be standard layouts as part of DTP software. However, you are not allowed to use these in your Higher Graphic Communication course.

Websites and tablet layouts can be animated and have transitions between each of the pages in the structure. They can also contain links to allow a user to purchase the product being advertised immediately.

It is commonplace for presentation and rendering software to be used to place 3D rendered models into suitable environments.

GO! Assignment Advice

Producing the thumbnails for your DTP work electronically will help you show clarity in your planning. It will also take less time for you to develop your thumbnail into the final layout. This is a big advantage in your timed assignment.

Chapter 2

Graphic Tools and Techniques

You will learn

- Knowledge and understanding of computer-aided techniques
- Preliminary graphics – manual techniques
- Digital capture/input and output techniques and devices
- Cloud computing
- Image file types
- Features of printed publications
- Digital advertising

- The paperless office
- Remote working
- Safe working practices when using DTP
- The impact of growing DTP software use
- Internet advertising
- CAD animation
- CAD simulation
- 3D printing

Knowledge and understanding of computer-aided techniques

Computers have a growing role in the production of the different types of technical drawing needed when designing new products or buildings.

Graphic tablets and stylus pens allow freehand sketching and rendering to be carried out using a computer. 3D computer-aided design (CAD) software allows realistic computer models to be created, edited and tested. Testing can take the form of analysis of machining processes to check before a physical model is made whether a component can be made without any issues or to test that parts like gears actually fit together. We can simulate how materials perform when forces are applied to them. For example, we can test if a part will break when placed under stress based on the properties of the material applied to it using the 3D CAD software. Will a part break when it is doing what it is designed to do based on the material applied to it using the 3D CAD software? This is called finite element analysis (FEA). We can also use the 3D CAD model to test computational fluid dynamics (CFD). This can be used to test how fluid in a hydraulic system flows or how airflow affects the aerodynamics of a component.

All of this means that many checks can be carried out before a physical model is made. This speeds up the design process and reduces the costs incurred by a design company.

Promotional drawings are also produced using powerful computer software to give photo-quality renders that can be controlled and edited better than actual photographs. These images can then be imported into a range of advertising publications, to produce a branded package of promotional material to help sell the products or buildings.

Desktop publishing

Many home computers come with DTP packages already installed. A professional standard DTP software package offers the user the ability to produce high-quality DTP documents. Photo editing software can also be used to help prepare images for presentations.

Video editing software can be used to communicate various types of technical graphics to an audience. This can be done using the same principles applied when producing DTP presentations.

Computer-aided design and computer-aided drawing

As 3D CAD packages have evolved and improved over the years with advances in computing technology, the role that this software plays has also changed.

Older 2D computer-aided drawing packages simply allowed a draughtsperson to complete production drawings on a computer using the same techniques as they would have used on a drawing board.

Modern 3D CAD software packages offer the user far more scope for producing and developing a product throughout the graphic design process. CADCAM techniques can be used to manufacture 3D products directly from 3D CAD models. Virtual reality scenarios and animations can be created to show particular technical details of a product, such as how moving parts operate, or to carry out material and strength tests.

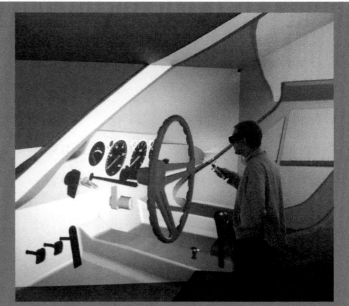

A scientist examines a projection of a Melkus RS 1000 racing car using a 3D CAD model and an interactive virtual reality scene.

Preliminary graphics – manual techniques

It is common for a graphic designer to begin the creative process using manual techniques.

A graphic designer will be able to produce high-quality sketches using the graphic equipment shown here. Indeed, **manual techniques** can be used to give a very lifelike indication of how a **proposed design** will look.

Often used alongside marker pens, correction pens are a useful and simple tool to create white edges for highlights.

You will be able to view online tutorials from a number of different YouTube channels to help you build up your sketching and rendering skills. The following examples show a combination of manual graphics using traditional graphic design mediums and electronic methods of sketching and rendering. This is not an exhaustive list but will give you a start:

- Drawing & Painting – The Virtual Instructor
- Paul Priestley
- TheSketchMonkey
- Spencer Nugent
- The Design Sketchbook
- Robert Laszlo Kiss
- SketchBook.

Drawing pens can be used to produce quick sketches and can also be used to add some simple rendering details, shadows and reflections.

Professional graphic design marker pens can be used to render preliminary sketches and give a very realistic image. They are especially useful for showing metals and plastics, but can also be used to show wooden materials.

High-quality graphic design colour pencils are used alongside marker pens to create the finished render. They can also be used on their own to create lifelike renders of an item, so a client can gauge what their product will look like when taken forward through the graphic design process.

🔵 GO! Assignment Advice

Practise using these graphic media during your studies to prepare for your assignment.

Digital capture/input and output techniques and devices

Handheld scanners

Modern handheld scanners are cheap to buy and easy to use. When used properly, they can produce high-quality scans very quickly. Their big advantage over flatbed scanners is that they are portable. They use memory cards to store the images until they can be transferred onto a computer.

Flatbed scanners

Flatbed scanners are useful for producing high-quality scans, as the original image or text is held completely still whilst being scanned. This type of scanner often comes as part of a home inkjet printer.

Laser printers

Laser printers give high-quality printouts using a CMYK format. They are becoming more affordable all the time for home use. Schools tend to use all-in-one copy, scan and print machines, which can be used to create pdf files of paper documents. This can help to reduce the physical storage space required for larger documents.

Graphics tablets

Used with a stylus pen, graphics tablets allow hand-produced sketches to be entered immediately onto a computer. This is far better than using a mouse to sketch and render with. It can be expensive to buy a good quality tablet, but they are coming down in price. Other handheld tablet devices can be used in the same way with rendering apps such as Autodesk Sketchbook or Adobe Photoshop Sketch.

Keyboard

A keyboard is used to input text. It is a basic but essential tool.

Monitor

All of the CAD models and DTP work are displayed on a monitor. When completing graphic projects, a larger, high-resolution monitor is preferable in order to display the images at a high quality.

Mouse

A mouse is needed when using 3D CAD or DTP software. The middle button on the mouse is a vital tool when using CAD, so it is important that you use a mouse that has one or a suitable alternative. (Any good quality computer mouse will have one.)

Projector

Projectors can be used to display work, animations or videos on a large screen to allow lots of people to view them.

Drum plotter

Drum plotters allow large drawings to be printed. The paper is moved back and forth through the printer by rollers. The printer head, which uses pens to produce line drawings, moves along the motorised axis.

Wide format inkjet printers like the one shown below allow large images to be printed for posters or banners. The rolls of paper used can be very long and the width of paper is limited by the size of the drum, which can be up to a few metres wide.

Sublimation printers

Sublimation printers can be used to print onto a variety of materials. They can be used to print onto a substrate, which can then be heat pressed onto soft advertising banners, T-shirts, rulers and mugs, amongst other items.

The sublimation printer shown on the right can be used to print a graphic that can then be transferred onto 3D items, such as mugs.

Portable storage facilities

Portable storage devices include USB flash drives and portable hard drives. They allow the user to save their work, take it with them and open the files on any computer in order to continue their work or to showcase it to others.

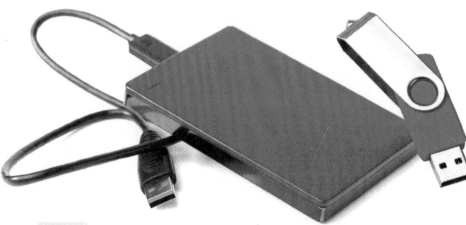

Email

Email can be used to share files immediately with anyone else anywhere in the world. Anyone with Internet access has free email services available to them, making this a time-efficient and environmentally friendly method of communication.

Cloud storage

Cloud storage offers the user a method of storing their work without having the need for any physical storage devices. Cloud storage has the added benefit of giving the user access to their work from any computer in the world that is connected to the Internet. The amount of cloud storage offered by companies differs, but can be large enough to suit any individual or organisation.

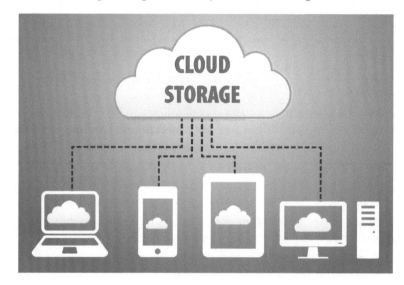

Cloud storage also provides a useful method of backup storage. It can be set to automatically sync with the contents of a hard drive or network to prevent data loss through disk or system corruption.

There are many different cloud storage options and some people will choose to keep the different types of files they have with different companies to improve their personal online security.

Cloud computing

Cloud computing has many uses and is improving as the technology that supports it improves. In computing, the term 'cloud' means 'Internet', so this is all about using computer programs over the Internet.

Traditionally, any programs or files that a user runs on their computer would have to have been installed onto their computer first.

This is called local storage and computing. Cloud computing allows programs to be run remotely over a network that is connected to the Internet, usually through WiFi.

There are some advantages and disadvantages when using cloud computing and cloud apps:

Advantages

- Computers designed solely for cloud computing can be cheaper than desktop or laptop machines. This is because they require less hard drive memory for programs and files as everything is either run from, or stored onto, the cloud.
- Individuals are able to use programs on any device, wherever they are.
- Only the programs that are required need to be paid for and used, instead of the other packages that come preinstalled on a computer or laptop.
- Companies can pay a subscription to a software producer rather than a large initial cost followed by additional costs for software updates.
- The most up-to-date version of the software will always be available as it is run from one central server.

Disadvantages

- A fast and reliable Internet connection is required to run cloud computing apps. A slow or inconsistent Internet connection will make cloud computing challenging.
- Connection charges to high-speed Internet connections can be expensive. This is especially true for companies that rely on this service. They can spend lots of money on their connection and any downtime from the Internet will lead to a lack of productivity.
- There can also be issues over who owns the rights to anything created or stored in the cloud.

Cloud computing is still developing. It is a system that allows portable access to apps as long as there is an Internet connection. Time and investment will result in lots of technological developments taking place to improve the current service. Some schools are investing in cloud computing so that each student can work with a computer in every classroom. Many companies are successfully using cloud computing systems. Many 3D CAD platforms are now being developed as cloud based. This means that the computers of the end user don't have to be as powerful because much of the calculation previously done using the RAM of the user's computer is now done in the cloud.

GO! Exam Tip

Cloud computing is a developing technology that is likely to feature in your exam.

Image file types

There are two main file types for images: raster files and vector files. Each type has its own advantages and disadvantages.

Raster graphics (tiff, jpg, png, bmp, gif, psd)

Raster graphics are created using a series of coloured pixels or squares. They can be created and edited using common photo editing packages such as GIMP (available as a free download), Photoshop, Affinity Photo or Paint. They tend to be used for photographs and artistic illustrations as colours can be blended to soften the change from one colour to the next. The quality of a raster file is measured in pixels per inch (ppi). The higher this number, the better quality raster file and the better quality image. The lower this ppi, the more pixelated, or blurry, an image will appear.

Advantages

- It is possible to change the quality setting for different types of output. Images for printed material will require a minimum of 300 dots per inch. Web-based images tend to be produced to around 72ppi or 96ppi to reduce the file size so they take less time to load.
- Suitable for photographs because they show detail in gradual colour changes.
- Can be edited using common photo editing programs.

Disadvantages

- Images can become pixelated when increased in size.
- Can be less suited for large-size print projects due to a loss in quality when resizing.
- Raster images produced to large dimensions with large amounts of detail have a large file size.
- Very complex raster images are difficult to convert to vector images.

You can see how this small raster image has become pixelated when resized.

Vector graphics (svg, dxf, eps, ai, cdr)

Vector graphics use mathematically defined areas to produce the shapes contained within the image. They can only be created using professional DTP and photo editing software such as Affinity Designer, CorelDraw, Adobe Illustrator or Inkscape (free to download). Gradient fills (where colours are gradually blended into one another) cannot be produced by a vector file; however, a raster gradient can be used within a vector graphic to create this effect if required.

Advantages

- Can be resized to a far larger image without any pixellation or loss of image quality.
- Vector images produced to a large physical size will have a small file size.
- It is easy to edit the colours of the various parts of a vector file (background, line, text) in DTP software.
- Can be used to create laser cutter tool paths.
- Clear and precise graphics can be produced. Vector files are especially suited to drawings and illustrations, company logos and technical drawings.
- Transparency can easily be applied to a background.
- Vector graphics can have a smaller file size than a raster file.
- Well suited to decals to be applied to physical products.

Disadvantages

- Cannot be used for photographs.
- Not suitable for images with gradual tonal changes with blended colour.
- Only specialised software packages can be used to create these type of graphics.
- Some software that edits these types of graphics can be expensive although some packages can be downloaded for free.

When this svg file is resized, there is no loss of sharpness.

> **GO! Exam Tip**
>
> You are likely to be asked to compare raster and vector files and to identify why one would be used in place of another in a given scenario.

GRAPHIC TOOLS AND TECHNIQUES

Features of printed publications

When printing on a commercial scale, it is important to be able to check if the process is set up properly and the printing machines are printing accurately. In order to do that, a number of check marks are printed at the side of the paper, outside the publication. These will be trimmed off before the publication is bound.

Colour printing typically uses ink of four colours: cyan, magenta, yellow and key (black).

Register marks

Registration is the name given to creating perfectly matched, overlapping colours on a page. When printing using the CMYK method, there will be a CMYK printing register mark visible, which allows it to be checked.

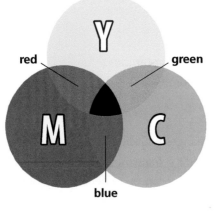

CMYK refers to the four layers of colour that are applied separately in the printing process. It stands for cyan, magenta, yellow and key (black). The colours must be aligned properly otherwise the printed images will appear distorted.

When two of the CMY 'primaries' are combined, the resulting 'secondary' mixtures are red, green and blue. If all three are combined, black is produced.

The reason for using black in a print product is to produce a true black. In theory, combining cyan, magenta and yellow in equal amounts will give black. However, combining the three colours does not, in practice, produce a true black. Mixing CMY gives a colour called process black. This is not a particularly dark black so black ink is used to allow this darker black to be produced.

When the registration is perfectly matched then the register mark will be clear and precise. When it is not, then the coloured circles will be printed in different places.

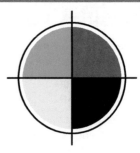

You can see how the registration mark on the left is misaligned, indicating a mistake in the application of the CMYK layers.

Colour bars

Colour bars are printed outside the trim area and are used to check the accuracy of the colours being printed in the document.

Crop marks

Crop marks are small marks at the corners of the finished page that show where the paper should be trimmed before binding. The term 'bleed area' describes the part of the paper outside the crop marks to which images or features are printed. This ensures that these features are printed to the full extent of the finished page. The bleed area is removed when the pages are trimmed before binding.

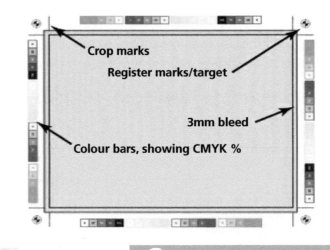

Crop marks

Register marks/target

3mm bleed

Colour bars, showing CMYK %

Print run

The print run is the number of copies of a newspaper or magazine that are printed at one time.

Digital advertising

Many adverts are displayed using digital formats. These digital adverts can be shown in a variety of places, from football stadiums to bus stops, using permanent or portable displays.

Digital adverts offer many different advantages to advertisers:

- It is environmentally friendly to display promotional layouts on digital displays as ink and paper are not required.
- Adverts can be changed regularly, cheaply and quickly.
- Adverts can use moving images to attract attention.
- Different adverts can be shown on the same display and flip through to have greater impact and advertise more products.
- Displays can be emailed to different venues, cutting down on delivery costs.

There are also some drawbacks to these digital platforms:

- The displays use electricity.
- Digital boards have to be transported around the country to allow the promotional work to be displayed.
- Consumers cannot take a hard copy of these adverts home for reference at a later date.

GO! Exam Tip

With the widespread presence of mobile phones and tablets, and the increasing amount of digital advertising space becoming available, digital advertising is a large and modern area of graphic communication and, as such, is likely to feature in your exam.

The paperless office

One of the major benefits to industry and the environment of the use of computers, DTP software and the Internet has been the reduction in paper used. Important documents are saved onto disk and held on computer systems.

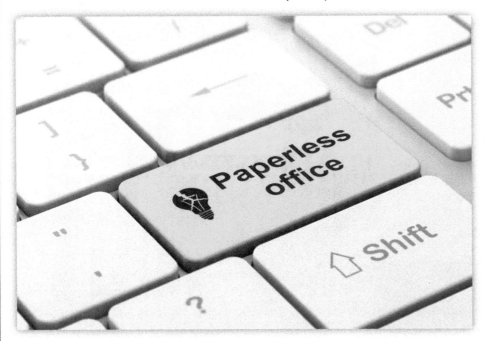

For DTP workplaces, this can be applied to almost all the work produced. Very little work is now produced by hand during the process of developing professional DTP publications. Thumbnail layouts are produced by computer software as it is quicker and allows high-quality work to be quickly produced all the way through the DTP development process, using structured grids and layouts.

Companies that can reduce the amount of paper used in their day-to-day work will save money and increase profit margins.

GO! Exam Tip

Revise the impact of the paperless office and remote working when preparing for your exam.

Remote working

DTP work can be shared immediately through the use of email systems. Employees can work from home or in separate offices on the same item of work.

Storing data on a single drive or server allows different people, in different places, to work on and update the same document. This allows companies to have international offices working on documents simultaneously to increase production and make use of the skills of a varied workforce.

All of this means that companies can become global as the world becomes connected via electronic, mobile and satellite networks. Anyone, from anywhere in the world, can communicate with anyone else using a variety of platforms.

Many news platforms and magazines are Internet-based and rely on DTP work to make their content look appealing. This opens exciting new markets and opportunities for a new range of employment prospects in this business sector.

Safe working practices when using DTP

If a business is to use DTP all day to produce documents, the welfare of its employees has to be protected.

Ergonomic factors have to be considered to look after a person's physical wellbeing. Ensuring that adjustable seating and footstools are provided and that wrist rests are used is essential.

Offices must be suitably lit with non-glare lighting and regular breaks must be taken from the computer screen to avoid headaches and eye strain. Other factors that have to be considered are tidy workspaces and arranging hardware and cables safely.

The impact of growing DTP software use

The introduction of DTP and computers has had a massive impact on the graphic communication industry and on the environment.

Since their introduction in design offices, computers have completely transformed the industry. Offices can now be paperless, with the use of graphics tablets, email, digital cameras and editing suites. In addition, the time it takes to produce publications has been shortened with the increased ease of editing through the use of computer software.

This has also been extended to the use of home computers and people creating their own DTP items, from calendars to cards.

A wide variety of DTP packages are available. These include:

- Adobe InDesign
- Affinity Publisher
- Corel Draw
- Microsoft Publisher
- Scribus
- Pages.

 **Exam Tip**

Revise the impact of the introduction and development of DTP software when preparing for your exam.

Internet advertising

Most websites sell advertising space on their pages to generate income. These adverts apply the same graphic elements and principles as other promotional layouts.

Website designers code the page to add links and create flashing or moving images to attract the attention of users. The presentation of the adverts is produced by a graphic designer for the website designer to use.

The most useful feature of advertising on websites is that web designers can use the information stored on your computer, phone or tablet to tailor the adverts you see. For example, if you have been searching for jackets, you will often see adverts for jackets on the websites you are visiting. This is obviously a huge advantage for advertisers and is why graphic design plays a large part in website design.

CAD animation

Computer animation can be used to help communicate how the moving parts of a 3D CAD model work together.

Animations allow a user to see how a product looks or moves. They are played and watched with no other input from the user.

Animations are used as a communication tool rather than a testing tool for the product. They are very useful in the promotional stages of a graphic presentation. The client will often wish to see an animated video to understand how moving parts work or how the various parts of an assembly are placed together.

CAD simulation

Simulations allow the user to interact with a product. The outcome of the simulation is dependent on the user's input. For example, a flight simulator can be used to train pilots without the risk of crashing a plane.

Simulations can also be used to test the strength of a product. Once a CAD model has had a material applied to it, the relevant part of the model will take on the engineering properties of that material. A load can then be applied to the model and the stress and strain measured and displayed. This is advantageous for a number of reasons:

- products can be tested for strength without lots of expensive physical models being tested to destruction
- changes to the design to strengthen failing parts can be made immediately
- a large number of different physical factors can be controlled, such as the temperature of the material and wind strength.

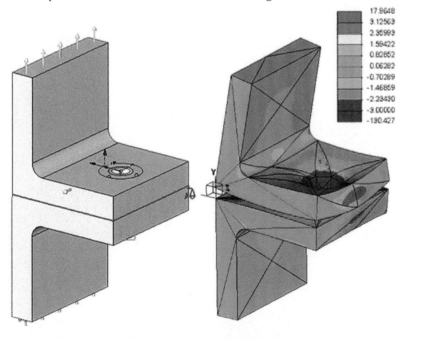

| 17.9648 |
| 3.12563 |
| 2.35993 |
| 1.59422 |
| 0.82852 |
| 0.06282 |
| -0.70289 |
| -1.46859 |
| -2.23430 |
| -3.00000 |
| -190.427 |

3D printing

3D printing is a growing area of the design process, which is having a large impact on manufacture. There is almost no limit to what can be produced using a 3D printer straight from a drawing. A variety of items, from tiny objects to buildings, are being produced using 3D printing techniques. Complex items with moving parts can be printed overnight and examined to see how they work quickly and easily, speeding up a traditionally time-consuming part of the design process.

Some companies are producing products to sell by 3D printing them. This reduces manufacturing costs for the companies involved. Once the 3D printer has been purchased, it can print any shape without any expensive tooling requirements.

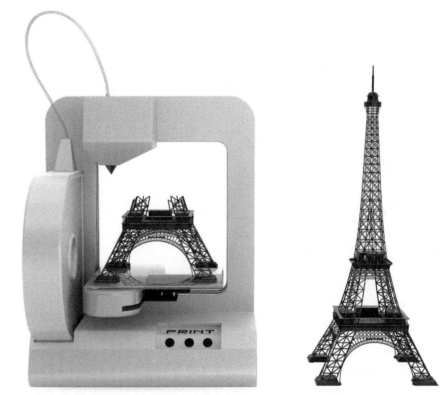

GRAPHIC TOOLS AND TECHNIQUES

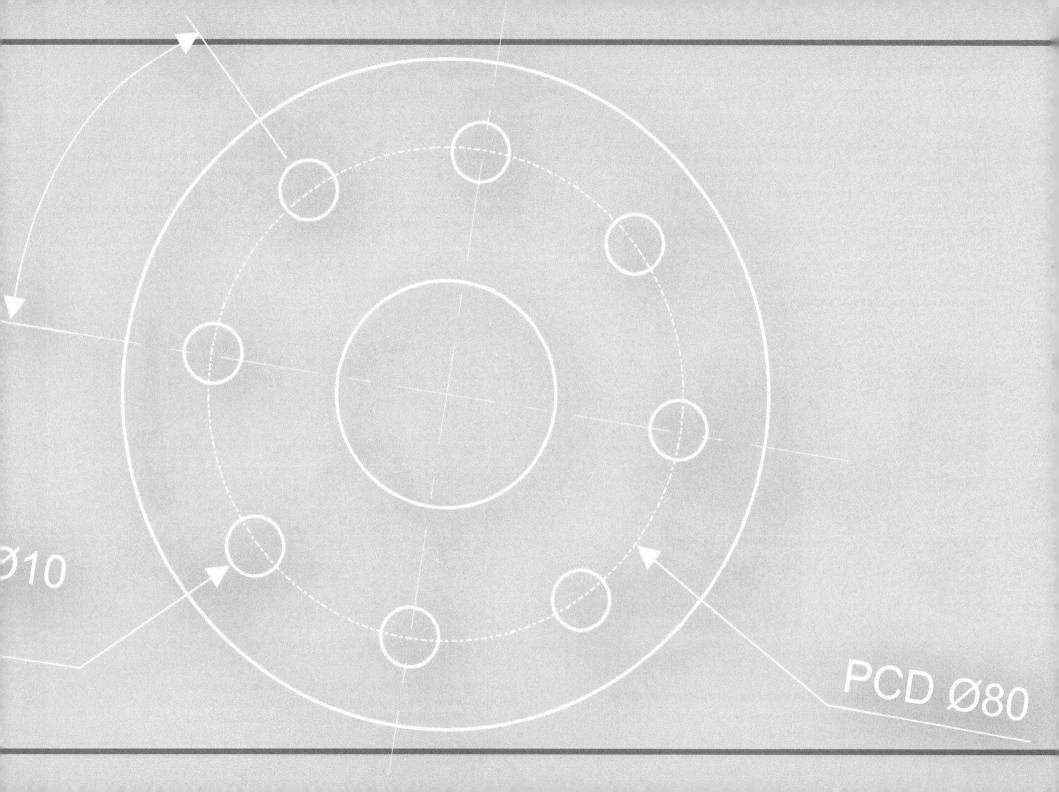

Chapter 3

Drawing, Dimensioning and Symbols

You will learn

- **Orthographic projection**
- **Dimensioning**
- **Title block**
- **Drawing scales**
- **Drawing sets**
- **Drawing symbols**
- **Tolerances**
- **Common symbols**

Orthographic projection

When laying out orthographic drawings, drawing standards should be consistently applied. In schools, the method used is third-angle projection.

Third-angle projection

It is vital to show the third-angle projection symbol on any drawing work you do, so that people reading the drawing know what projection method has been used.

Orthographic projection is a way of drawing different views of an object. In third-angle projection, the plan (top view) is drawn directly above the elevation (front view) and the end elevation (side view) is drawn directly to the right of the elevation.

The drawing below shows how a third-angle projection brings the three views together.

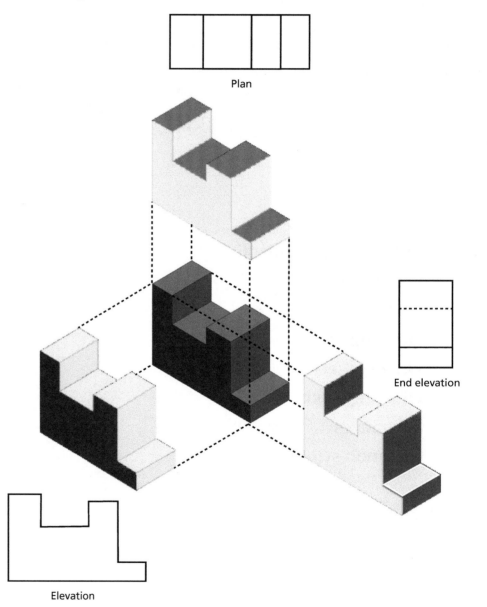

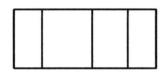

Plan

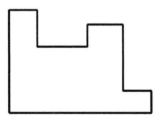

Elevation

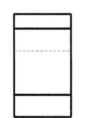

End elevation

Third-angle projection symbol

Plan

End elevation

Elevation

First-angle projection

First-angle projection is not used within Higher Graphic Communication, but you should be aware that it exists. It is the opposite of third-angle projection. The plan is shown below the elevation and the right-hand side view (end elevation) is shown on the left.

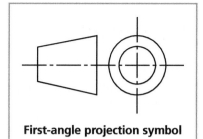

First-angle projection symbol

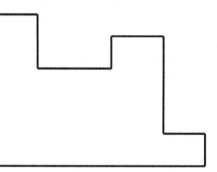

End elevation

Elevation

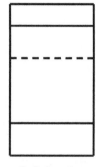

Plan

Line types

You need to know the different line types that are used in orthographic drawings.

The lines are all drawn to British Standards so that they can be understood by anyone who reads the drawing. This eliminates mistakes that could be expensive to fix or, more importantly, dangerous if translated to the end product.

GO! Assignment Advice

You are awarded marks for following British Standards throughout your assignment. Make sure you use the correct line types – these are easy marks to collect!

Construction line

Outline

Hidden detail line

Centre line

Fold line

Cutting plane

Line of symmetry

Dimensioning

Vertical dimensions are always written in the middle and on the left-hand side of the dimension line.

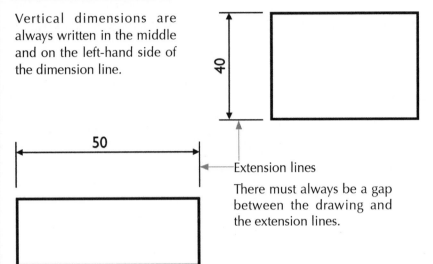

Extension lines

There must always be a gap between the drawing and the extension lines.

Horizontal dimensions are always written in the middle and above the dimension line.

Chain dimensioning

Chain dimensions follow each other in a line.

Auxiliary dimensions

Auxiliary dimensions are not required on a drawing for any technical reason, but help to make lengths more obvious.

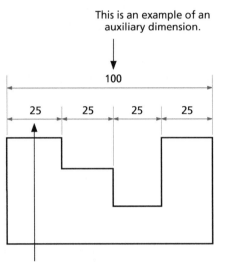

This is an example of an auxiliary dimension.

GO! Assignment Advice

You must use the correct British Standards method of dimensioning for both your preliminary and production drawings.

Chain dimensioning is used to show the length of each step in this shape.

Parallel dimensioning

Parallel dimensions are shown above and below each other. They are used when dimensioning from a datum point. The advantage of using this type of dimensioning is that it is more accurate when tolerances are important.

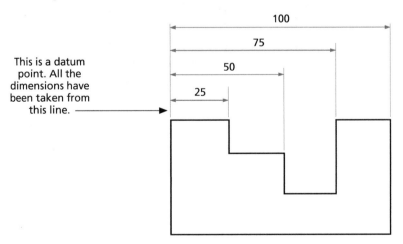

This is a datum point. All the dimensions have been taken from this line.

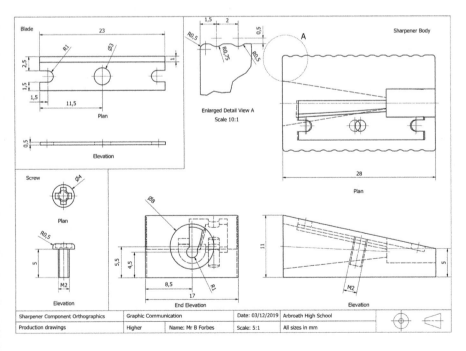

Running dimensioning

Running dimensions show the sizes from the datum line. The values are not positioned in the centre of the dimension line in this method, to help show that all the dimensions are taken from the datum line. It also helps to differentiate running dimensions from the other methods.

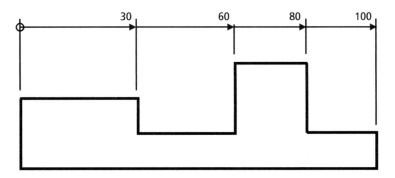

Angular dimensioning

Angles need to be dimensioned to show their slope. This is important to allow tapered objects to be manufactured accurately.

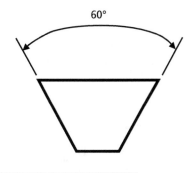

🔵 GO! Exam Tip

Dimensioning is vital as sizes are required to manufacture a product. British Standards must be followed when applying dimensions to a drawing. You must know the term for each of these dimensioning styles for your exam.

Pitch circle diameter

Pitch circle diameter allows a group of circles on the same diameter to be dimensioned clearly. The diameter of the circle that all the circles sit on is shown, as is the diameter of each individual circle and the angles between the circles.

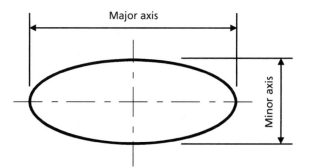

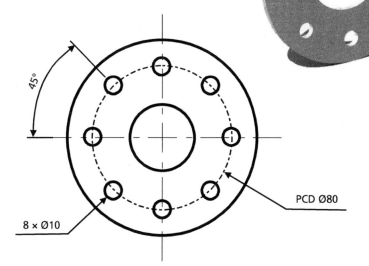

PCD Ø80

8 × Ø10

45°

Dimensioning an ellipse

An ellipse has two different measurements to be dimensioned: the major axis and minor axis.

Major axis

Minor axis

Dimensioning a circle

There are three acceptable methods you can use to dimension a circle. You should choose the most suitable one for the drawing you are dimensioning. Remember that the purpose of dimensions is to clearly show the technical details of a drawing, so you should pick the method that allows you to do this. The symbol Ø means diameter and must be positioned before the numerical size whenever you are dimensioning a circle.

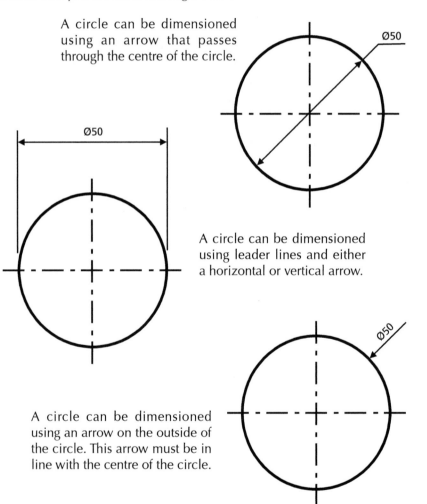

A circle can be dimensioned using an arrow that passes through the centre of the circle.

Ø50

A circle can be dimensioned using leader lines and either a horizontal or vertical arrow.

A circle can be dimensioned using an arrow on the outside of the circle. This arrow must be in line with the centre of the circle.

Dimensioning a radius

There are two ways of dimensioning a radius. As with dimensioning circles, you should choose the method that most clearly shows the radius. The symbol R is used to show a radius.

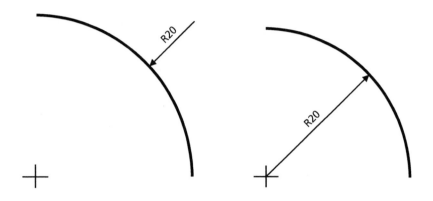

Dimensioning small features

When dimensioning small features, placing the dimension arrow between projection lines may create a drawing that is difficult to read. In order to clarify the dimensions of small features, any of the methods shown below can be used.

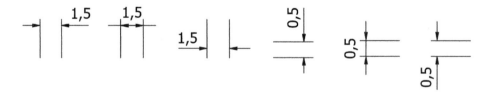

Dimensioning a hexagon

There are two ways that hexagons can be dimensioned: either across the flats (AF) or across the corners (AC).

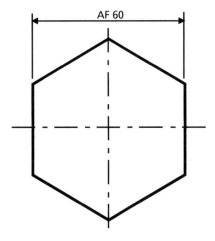

AF 60

The British Standards symbol for across the flats is AF. The number indicates the size of the hexagon in millimetres.

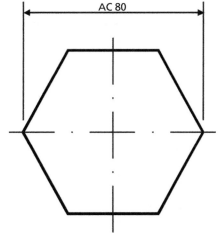

AC 80

The British Standards symbol for across the corners is AC. The number indicates the size of the hexagon.

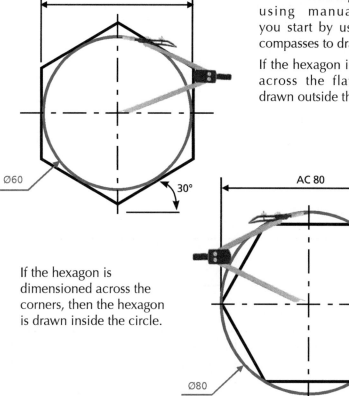

AF 60

Ø60

30°

AC 80

Ø80

60°

When drawing a hexagon using manual methods, you start by using a pair of compasses to draw a circle.

If the hexagon is dimensioned across the flats, then it is drawn outside the circle.

If the hexagon is dimensioned across the corners, then the hexagon is drawn inside the circle.

Dimensioning a square

As all the sides of a square are of equal length, there is a British Standards convention to apply that makes dimensioning a square more efficient and clearer to read.

The □ symbol identifies a square, while the number identifies the length of the sides of the square.

□ 60

Title block

A title block is a label added to a drawing that contains relevant information. This information is needed to be able to read production drawings properly, so that the product they are showing can be manufactured.

A title block should contain:

1. The name of the drawing.

2. The name of the person who produced the drawing.

3. The date the drawing was produced on.

4. The scale of the drawing.

5. The projection symbol.

6. The unit of measurement used for the drawing.

7. The title of the project.

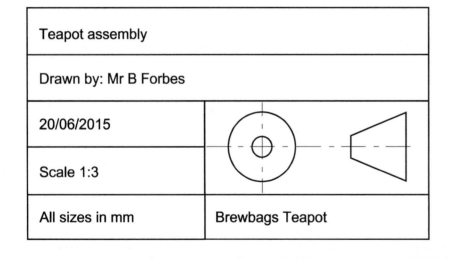

Teapot assembly	
Drawn by: Mr B Forbes	
20/06/2015	
Scale 1:3	
All sizes in mm	Brewbags Teapot

Exam Tip

You need to be able to identify the details found in a title block and know how to work out scales for drawings.

Assignment Advice

Create a blank production drawing sheet at the beginning of the course. Use this sheet for all the production drawings you produce while studying Higher Graphic Communication, including in the assignment.

Drawing scales

Drawing scales are used regularly in drawing sets. They tell you how much smaller or larger a drawing is than the real-life object.

They can be calculated very easily. A scale of 2:1 means double size, while a scale of 1:2 is half size. To work it out, replace the colon (:) with a dividing line. For example:

2:1 becomes $\frac{2}{1}$ which means the size is doubled.

1:2 becomes $\frac{1}{2}$ which means the size is halved.

When an object is shown at full size, the scale is 1:1.

There are three main factors that affect the scale used for an object:

1. The size of the paper the object is drawn on.

2. The size of the object itself.

3. The amount of detail that needs to be shown.

Often you will see enlargement scales of 50:1, 20:1 and 2:1.

You will also see reduction scales of 1:50, 1:200 and 1:1250 used in building sets for floor plans, site plans and location plans, respectively.

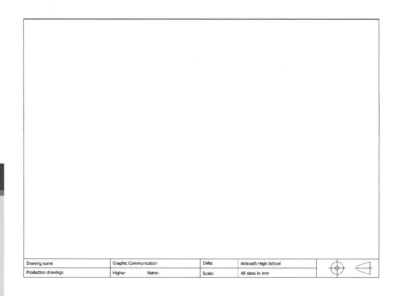

Drawing name	Graphic Communication	Date:	Arbroath High School	
Production drawings	Higher Name:	Scale:	All sizes in mm	

Use of appropriate drawing scales

Different items will have to be drawn at a range of different scales. You have to be able to select the most relevant scale for your needs.

Larger items will need to be drawn at smaller scales, while smaller items often have to be scaled up to clearly see the detail.

The size of the paper used to produce a drawing is also a contributing factor in selecting the scale. Larger sheets of paper allow a larger drawing to be printed than smaller sheets.

The drawing below shows the parts of a lamp drawn at different scales in order to show the detail in them. This allows the engineer to view the smaller and larger parts of the lamp clearly, so that it can be manufactured.

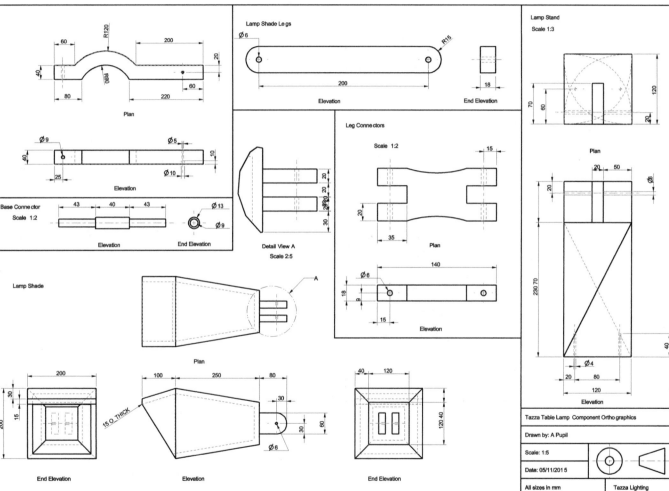

Drawing sets

Drawing sets contain all the drawings necessary to complete a building project. A drawing set will include drawings to clearly show the layout of the buildings and where they will be situated.

There are three drawings used to show this. These are listed below along with the scale they are drawn at:

1. Location plan – 1:1250

2. Site plan – 1:200

3. Floor plan – 1:50

Location plan

A location plan shows the position of a building within a wider area. Surrounding streets and buildings are shown.

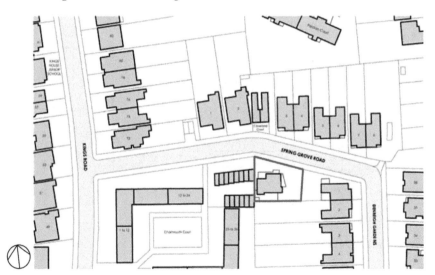

Site plan

A site plan shows where a building is going to be built and its immediate surrounding area. Some of the details shown in a site plan are:

- drainage
- gas pipe work
- electrical supply cables
- telephone and TV cables
- trees and hedges
- slopes (called swales) to take rainwater away from the house.

Below is an example of a site plan. The arrow within the circle is the symbol used to indicate the direction of north on a map.

> **GO!** **Exam Tip**
>
> Make sure you know the scales used for floor plans, site plans and location plans.

> **GO!** **Exam Tip**
>
> You will need to know the symbols for these items for your exam.

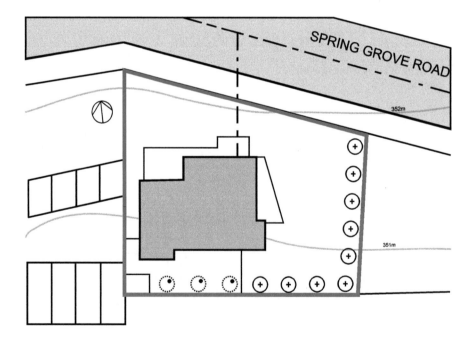

Floor plan

A floor plan shows the details of a layout of the floor in a building. Walls, windows, doors, sockets, switches, lamps, furniture and staircases are some of the items shown using this layout.

Ground Floor
Approx. 83.4 sq. metres (897.8 sq. feet)

Dining Room
4.00m x 4.00m
(13'1" x 13'1")

Kitchen
4.00m (13'1") max
5.00m (16'5")

Utility

Lounge
5.00m (16'5") excl bay
4.00m (13'1")

WC

Study
3.40m x 2.70m
(11'2" x 8'10")

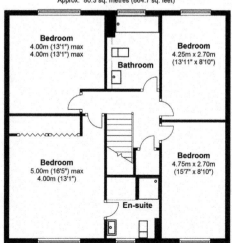

First Floor
Approx. 80.3 sq. metres (864.7 sq. feet)

Bedroom
4.00m (13'1") max
4.00m (13'1") max

Bathroom

Bedroom
4.25m x 2.70m
(13'11" x 8'10")

Bedroom
5.00m (16'5") max
4.00m (13'1")

Bedroom
4.75m x 2.70m
(15'7" x 8'10")

En-suite

Drawing symbols

Throughout these drawing sets you must use the correct British Standard symbols for any detail or item you show in them.

You will have access to a document produced by the SQA that contains all of the symbols that you need to know for all levels of Graphic Communication study. This document is called 'Graphic Communication – Standards and Conventions' and is available to download from the SQA website for Higher Graphic Communication.

The SQA publishes all of the symbols that you need to know for all levels of Graphic Communication. You can find these symbols in the course specification for Higher Graphic Communication. You can download and/or view this from the SQA website for Higher Graphic Communication.

It is imperative that you use only the terms and words stated in the Higher Graphic Communication Course Specification for each of the items.

GO! Exam Tip

You must state the exact term used by British Standards for these symbols in order to be awarded the marks in the exam. The reference document produced by the SQA contains the correct names.

Drawing symbols are used in plans for buildings. They allow the materials and details of a building to be communicated to builders and engineers. They follow British Standards and are always drawn the same way so that people can understand them.

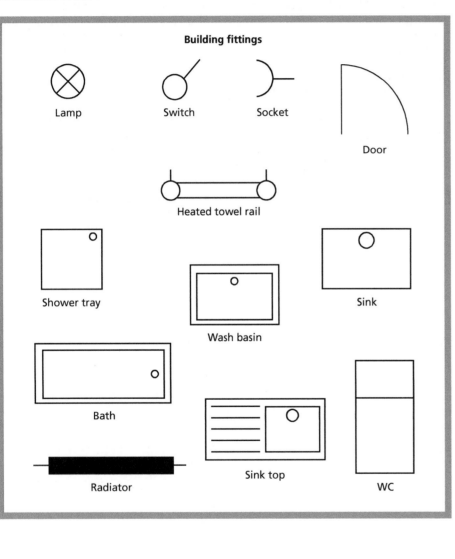

Building fittings

Lamp

Switch

Socket

Door

Heated towel rail

Shower tray

Wash basin

Sink

Bath

Radiator

Sink top

WC

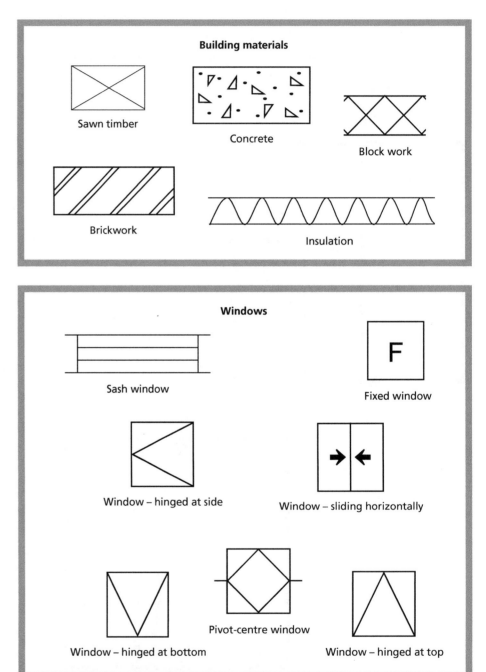

Building materials

Sawn timber

Concrete

Block work

Brickwork

Insulation

Windows

Sash window

Fixed window

Window – hinged at side

Window – sliding horizontally

Window – hinged at bottom

Pivot-centre window

Window – hinged at top

Exam Tip

If asked to identify these symbols in your exam, you must use the exact terms in order to be awarded the marks. These symbols and their terms are all described in the course specification document. Check this each year for updates and make sure that you use the terms as they are described in the Higher Graphic Communication Course Specification document.

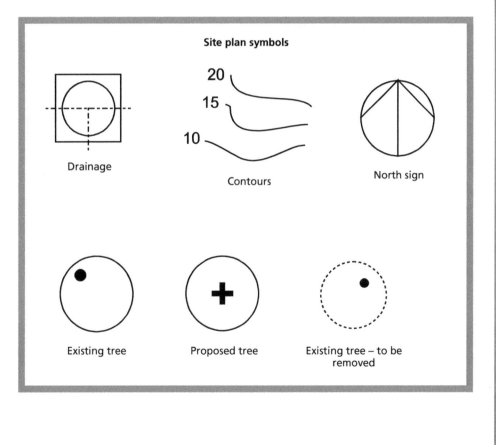

Site plan symbols

Drainage

20
15
10

Contours

North sign

Existing tree

Proposed tree

Existing tree – to be removed

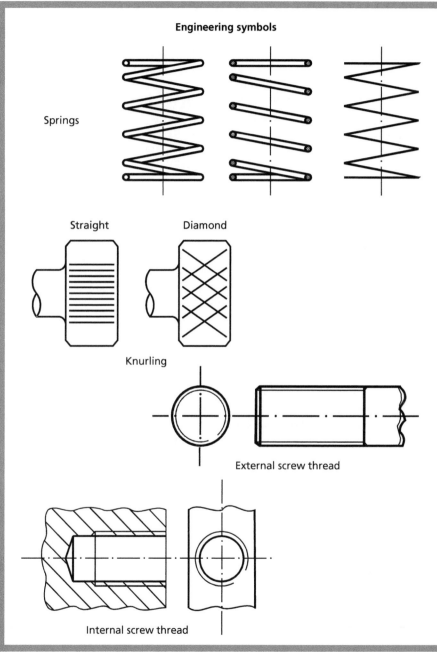

Engineering symbols

Springs

Straight

Diamond

Knurling

External screw thread

Internal screw thread

Tolerances

In practice, it is not possible to manufacture products to the exact dimensions displayed on an engineering drawing. The accuracy depends largely on the manufacturing process used and the care taken to manufacture the product. A tolerance value shows the manufacturing department the maximum variation permissible from the dimension.

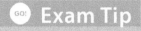

Exam Tip

Take a calculator into your exam to help calculate tolerances.

Each dimension on a drawing must include a tolerance value. This can appear either as:

- a general tolerance value applicable to several dimensions, e.g. General Tolerance ± 0.5 mm
- a tolerance specific to that dimension.

There are two methods of tolerancing dimensions. These are symmetrical and asymmetrical tolerances.

Symmetrical tolerances

Symmetrical tolerances are used in instances when the dimensions of the manufactured object can be out by the same amount above or below the dimensioned size.

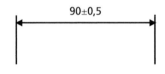

Asymmetrical tolerances

Asymmetrical tolerances are used when a size must be between two given dimensions. Note the comma used in the tolerance sizes.

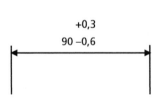

Tolerancing of individual linear dimensions

When it is important that individual dimensions are toleranced over and above the general tolerance for an object, the tolerance should be written as shown below. This shows the minimum and maximum sizes for the part clearly.

Note that the larger size limit is placed above the lower limit.

All tolerances should be expressed to the appropriate number of decimal places for the degree of accuracy intended from manufacturing, even if the value is a zero. For example:

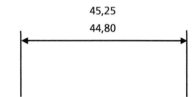

- 45,25 should be expressed as 45,25
- 44,8 should be expressed as 44,80

Functional and non-functional tolerances

Functional tolerances are essential to a component being manufactured correctly. The sizes indicated by these must be accurate for the product or part to work properly.

Non-functional tolerances are not as important as they do not play a critical role in the function of a part.

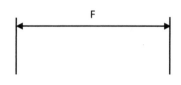

DRAWING, DIMENSIONING AND SYMBOLS

Common symbols

Using symbols to convey information is the crux of Graphic Communication. Using graphics to inform people has many advantages over literary methods. Information can be understood far quicker and people of any nationality can understand the message when it is communicated graphically.

Symbols are not restricted to engineering contexts. Storyboards can be produced to help people understand how something works. For example, how to operate a machine or toy. Road signs used across the UK since 1965 were developed by Margaret Calvert and Jock Kinneir to quickly convey information while people are driving on the roads.

THIS WAY UP

FRAGILE

HEAVY LIFT WITH CARE

Types of signs

One way
Mon–Sat 10am–4pm

A mandatory sign

A prohibition sign

A warning sign

A safe condition sign

The BSI kite mark

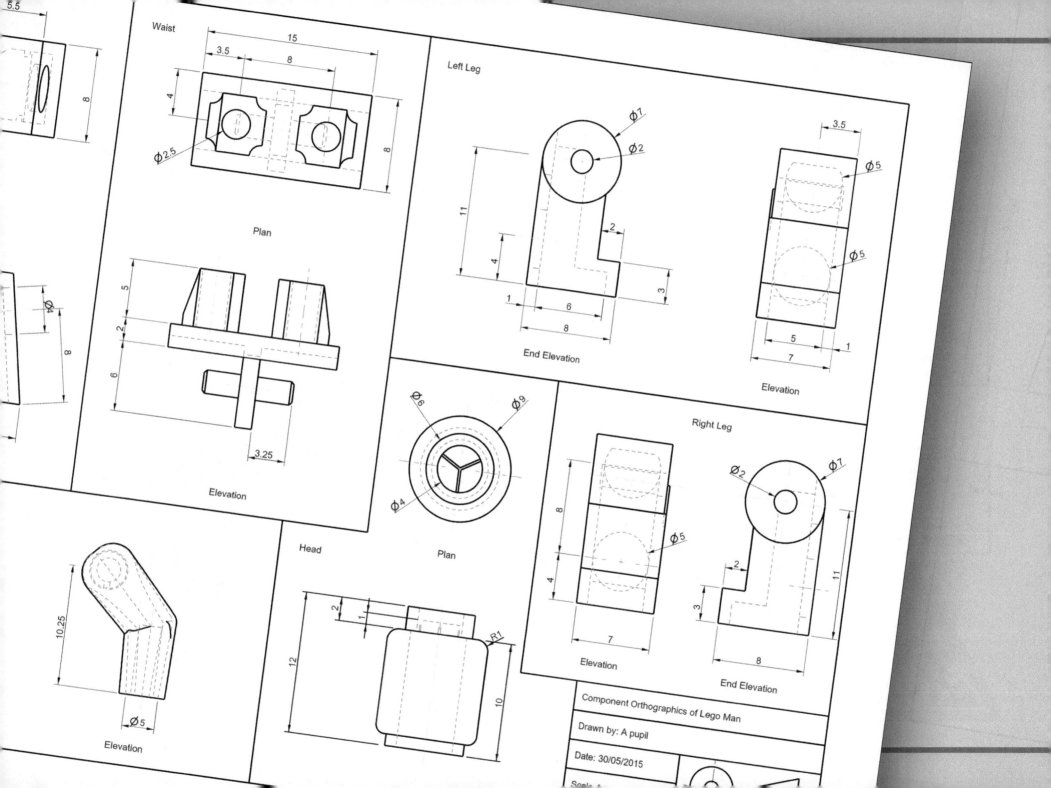

Waist

15
3.5
8
4
8
8
Ø2.5

Plan

5
2
6
3.25

Elevation

Left Leg

Ø7
Ø2
11
4
2
1
6
3
8

End Elevation

3.5
Ø5
Ø5
5
1
7

Elevation

Head

Ø6
Ø9
Ø4

Plan

2
1
12
R1
10

Right Leg

8
Ø5
4
7

Elevation

Ø2
Ø7
2
3
11
8

End Elevation

10.25
Ø5

Elevation

Ø4
8

5.5
8

Component Orthographics of Lego Man

Drawn by: A pupil

Date: 30/05/2015

Scale

Chapter 4

Technical Drawings

You will learn

- Orthographic projection
- Sectional views
- Full sectional views
- Half-sectional views
- Stepped sectional views
- Revolved sectional views
- Removed sectional views
- Part-sectional views
- Isometric views
- Assembly drawings
- Exploded views
- Auxiliary views
- Ellipses

- Tangency
- Interpenetration of cylinders
- Intersections of prisms
- True length and true shape
- Auxiliary views – using CAD
- Surface development
- Oblique views
- Planometric views
- Perspective views

Orthographic projection

Orthographic projection is the name given to the technical, dimensioned drawings that allow a product to be manufactured.

As discussed earlier in this book, you should use third-angle projection when producing orthographic drawings throughout your work in Higher Graphic Communication.

Component views are dimensioned. Component orthographic drawings show the views of the individual parts that fit together to build the item being drawn. Component orthographic views show all the dimensions, centre lines and technical detail required to allow each component to be manufactured.

Assembly views show each of the component parts drawn together to show how a product is assembled. Assembled views do not normally show dimensions, unless there are some sizes that are only relevant to the assembly views.

A title block is shown on each sheet containing production drawings to give some information about them.

The component orthographic views and a rendered view of the assembled figure are shown here.

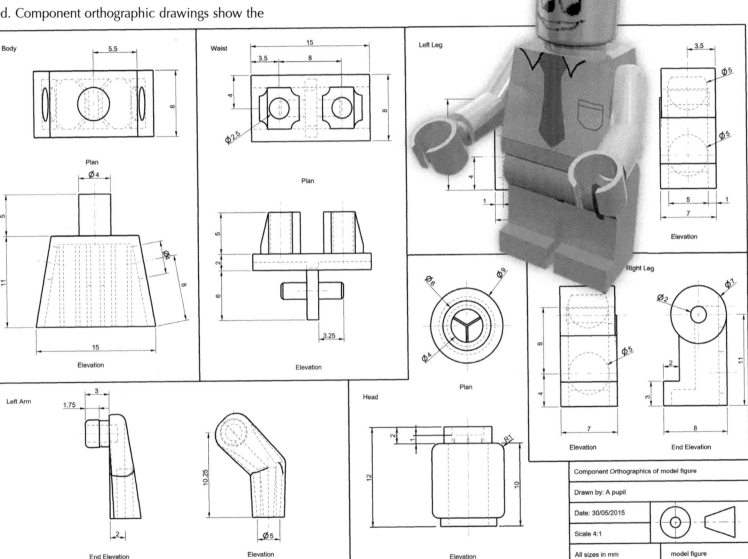

Sectional views

Sectional views are produced to show the internal detail of an object. They cut away part of an object and show what is left. No hidden detail is ever shown in a sectional view.

When a sectional view is made, a cutting plane is used to show where the cut has been made. The part behind the arrows is cut away.

This is a cutting plane.

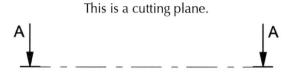

A cutting plane has a few features:

1. Thicker lines at the ends.

2. Arrows show the direction in which the section is to be viewed. Everything behind the arrows is removed.

3. Letters to label the cutting plane and sectional view. These are required as more than one cutting plane may be evident.

Hatching lines show where material is cut in a sectional view and should be drawn at 45°. They are drawn in different directions or with different spacing to show different materials or parts.

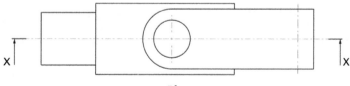

Plan

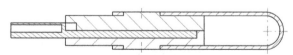

End Elevation   **Sectional Elevation on XX**

Herringbone

It is important that hatching lines on a sectional view do not meet each other to create a herringbone pattern, as this does not follow British Standards. An example of an incorrect herringbone pattern is shown here.

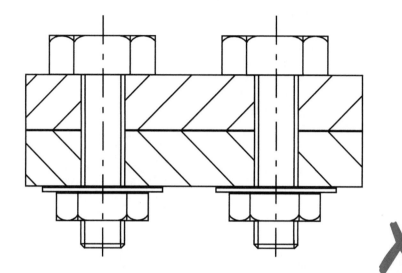

You can see from the drawing below the correct method of hatching two materials.

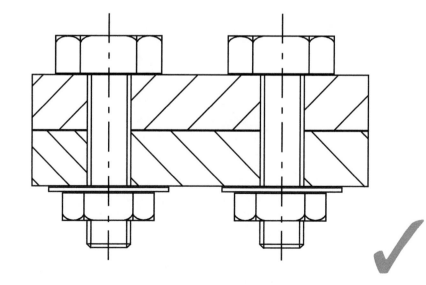

Full sectional views

Full sectional views cut all the way through an object.

The view here is a pictorial view of the model figure with a full section applied. The orthographic views of this are shown next to it.

You can see that the sectional view is labelled as **Sectional End Elevation on AA**. This identifies the view as the sectional view of the cutting plane labelled AA. It gets its name (AA in this case) from the two letters at the end of the cutting plane, in this example A and A. It still follows the same rules as the third-angle projection method, which is why it is referred to as a sectional end elevation.

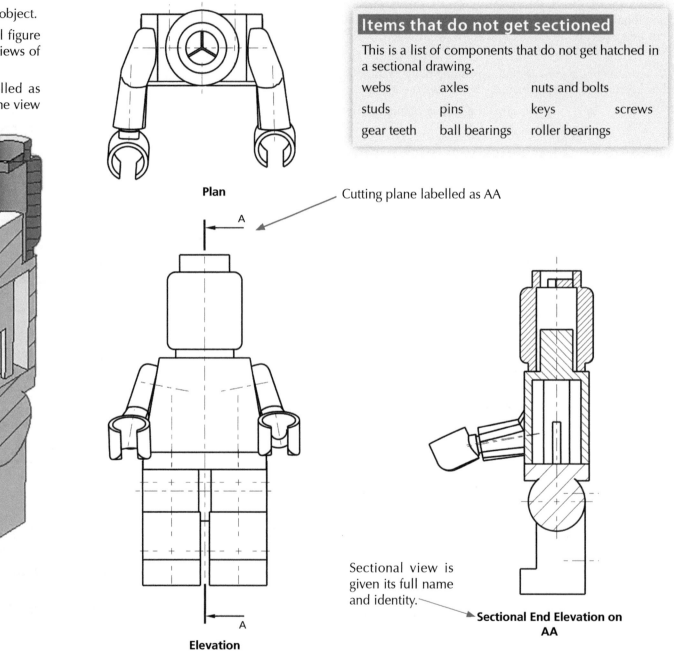

Plan

Cutting plane labelled as AA

A

Elevation

Sectional view is given its full name and identity.

Sectional End Elevation on AA

Half-sectional views

Half-sectional views cut away a quarter of the object. They are given the name 'half-section' as they cut away half of a full section.

Stepped sectional views

Stepped sectionals can also be called offset sections. They allow a cutting plane to change direction.

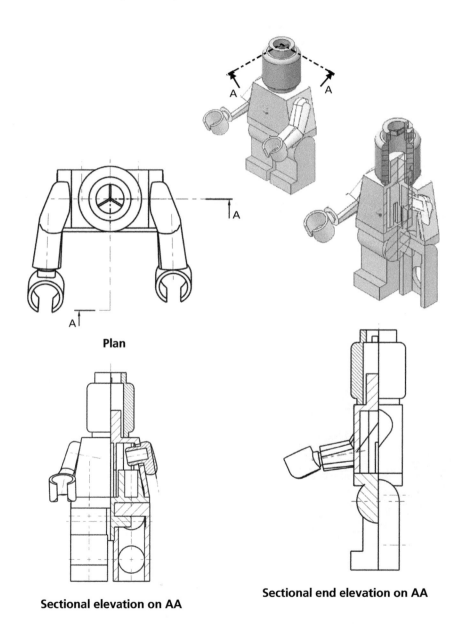

Plan

Sectional elevation on AA

Sectional end elevation on AA

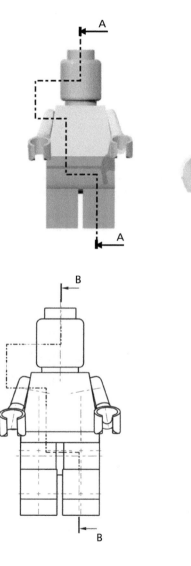

Elevation

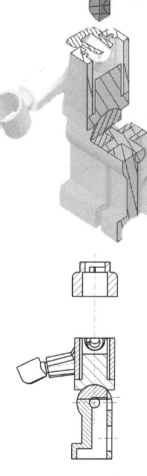

Sectional end elevation on BB

Revolved sectional views

Revolved sectional views show the sectional view within the elevation of an object. They are rotated around a centre line and at 90° to it. The sectional view is shown on top of the elevation.

These views are useful to save space and show the section of a long, constant-sectioned object.

Removed sectional views

Removed sectional views are similar to revolved sections, but are drawn outside of the original view. A cutting plane is used to show where the section is made.

They are used to show small details and to help with clear dimensioning where required. For this reason, they are often drawn in enlarged scale.

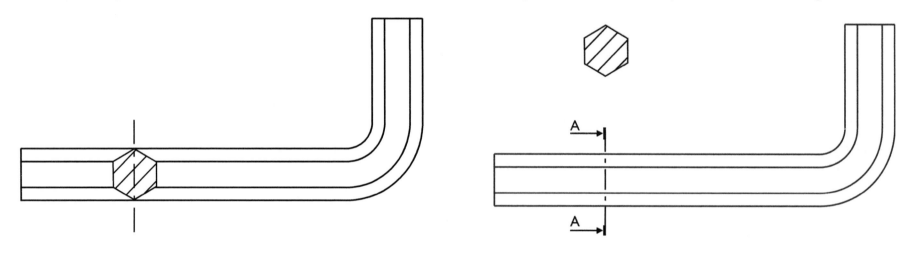

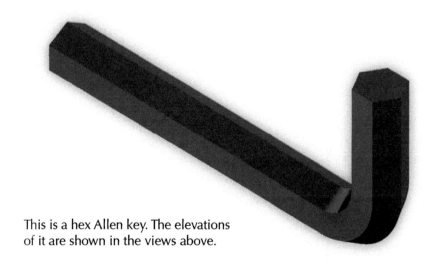

This is a hex Allen key. The elevations of it are shown in the views above.

Part-sectional views

Part-sectional views are used when only a small part of the internal shape of an object is required and a full or half-section may not be needed. You can define the outside of a part-section with a break line or a combination of a break line and a centre line.

The detail view of the part-sectional elevation of the model figure is shown below. A break line has been used to show the extent of the part-section applied.

Showing flat surfaces

Flat surfaces are shown using a cross. This is important as without this cross, they can seem to be round.

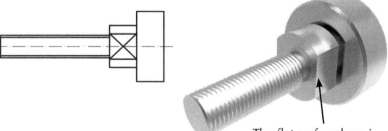

The flat surface here is shown as a cross on the orthographic view.

Showing a web

A web is a sloping bit of material added to an object in order to add strength. Webs are not hatched when sectioned to show them separately from the rest of the part.

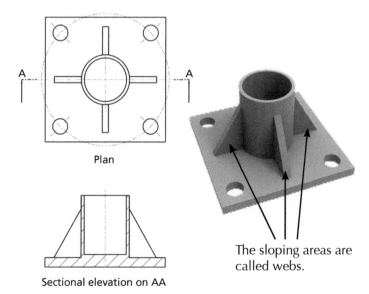

A — — — A

Plan

Sectional elevation on AA

The sloping areas are called webs.

Isometric views

Isometric views are a type of pictorial view. Specifically, an isometric view is drawn at 30° and 30° angles. They are often used to produce 3D views as they can show a realistic but technically structured view of a product.

30°   30°

Assembly drawings

Assembly drawings are produced when the various parts of a product are assembled together. As discussed earlier, these are not normally dimensioned but are important to show how an object is assembled.

At Higher level, you need to be able to produce assembly drawings that have a minimum of three parts. No hidden detail is shown in assembly drawings.

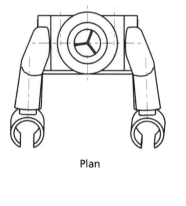

Plan

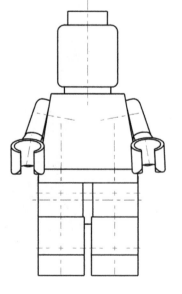

Elevation

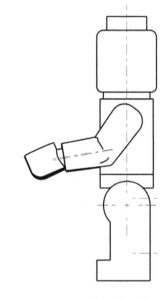

End elevation

Exploded views

Components must be exploded in the same plane as they will fit together in when assembled. Components must not overlap each other in an exploded view. Exploded views are often used in flat packs to show people how to build the furniture.

This type of view is included in the production part of a drawing set, as it adds value to the technical detail required to manufacture a product.

Exploded isometric view

Auxiliary views

An auxiliary view looks at an object from an angle. The rules of projection are still followed but instead of projecting horizontally, like you would for an end elevation, this projection takes place at an angle perpendicular (at right-angles) to an edge on the drawing.

This can be used to show particular parts of a drawing in more detail.

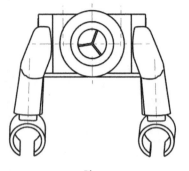

Plan

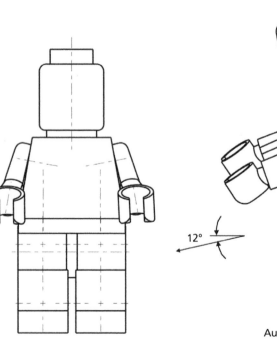

12°

Elevation

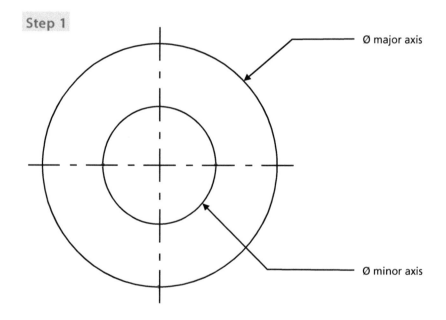

Auxiliary end elevation

Ellipses

Ellipses are shapes like squashed circles.

They are dimensioned using the technique shown with the major axis and minor axis.

To construct an ellipse on a computer, you use the ellipse tool. On paper, you need to draw two concentric circles, one with the diameter of the minor axis and the other with the diameter of the major axis.

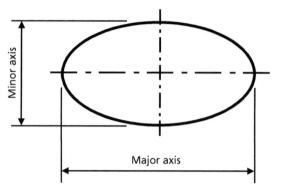

Minor axis

Major axis

Step 1

Ø major axis

Ø minor axis

Step 2

The next stage is to construct a clock face on the circles using lines at 30°.

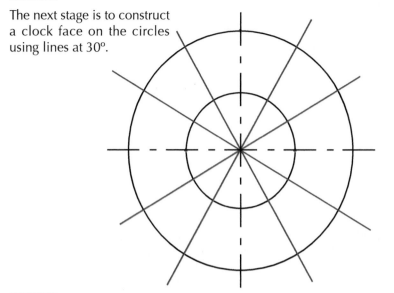

Step 4

Next, project lines from where the clock face intersects the inner circle vertically outwards.

Mark where these lines cross the horizontal lines with a dot.

You can remember this with the saying:

inside out, outside in.

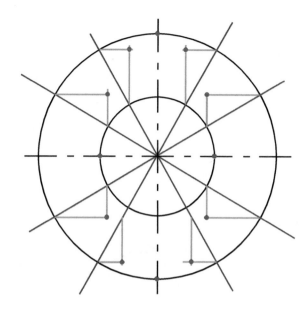

Step 3

Take horizontal lines from the points where the clock face lines cross the outer circle in towards the centre.

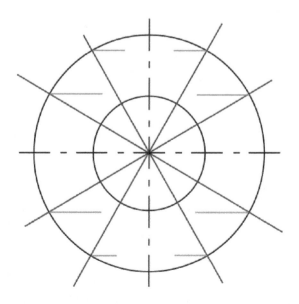

Step 5

You can draw the ellipse by joining the dots with a smooth freehand curve.

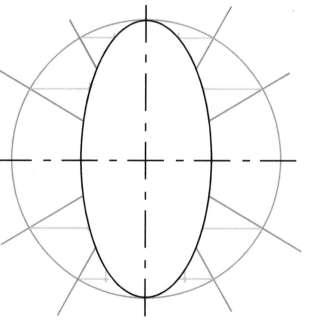

Tangency

Tangency is where a line or curve meets another curve at one point only.

Points of tangency can be found easily when using CAD software using the tangent snap.

When using a drawing board, tangency has to be calculated and found using manual techniques.

We can have tangency between a straight line and an arc and you will need to know about two types of tangency when working with circles.

1. Internal tangency – where a circle or arc is inside another.

2. External tangency – where the circles or arcs are outside each other.

Internal and external tangency location

To calculate where to draw an arc or circle that is tangent to another line or curve, you need to know the following two features:

1. Its radius or diameter.

2. The exact point for its centre.

For **internal tangency**, **subtract** the radii of the arcs or circles from each other.

For **external tangency**, **add** the radii together.

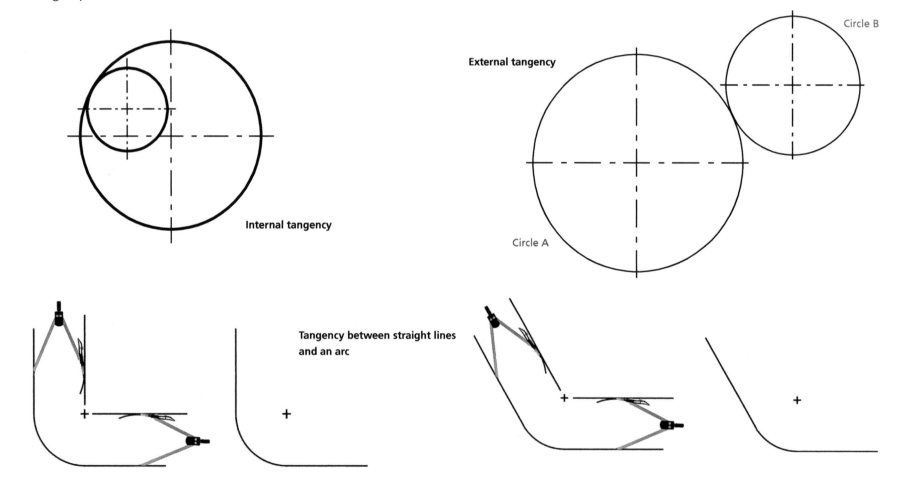

Internal tangency

External tangency

Circle B

Circle A

Tangency between straight lines and an arc

The shape shown here is the base for a gate nameplate. Tangency is used to create the arcs on the top and on the left- and right-hand sides.

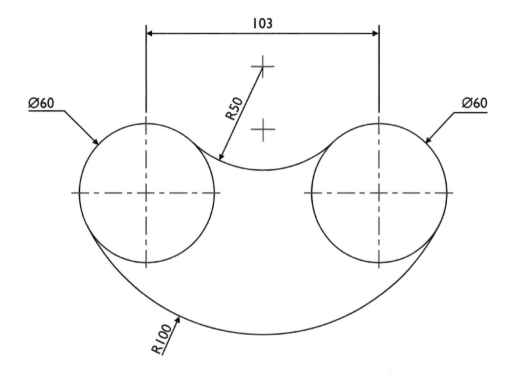

When drawing tangent arcs, you have to identify whether the arcs are inside or outside each other. Remember, if the arcs are outside each other, then add the radii. If the arcs are inside each other, then subtract the radii.

Drawing the first tangent arc

The first stage of drawing the tangent arc on the top of the nameplate is to find the centre of the arc.

The arcs are outside each other, so the radii must be added. With a pair of compasses set to 80 mm (30 mm (half the circle's diameter) plus the 50 mm radius of the tangent arc) draw two arcs, one from the centre of each circle.

Step 1

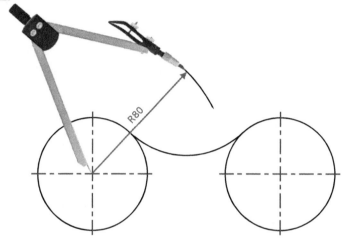

Step 2

Mark the centre point (where the arcs intersect) with a cross.

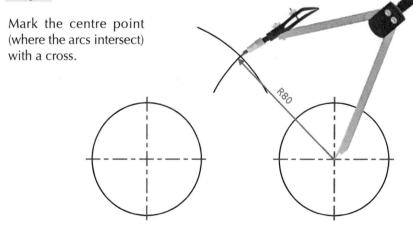

Step 3

The pair of compasses are then set to the correct radius of 50 mm and the tangent arc is drawn from the centre point created.

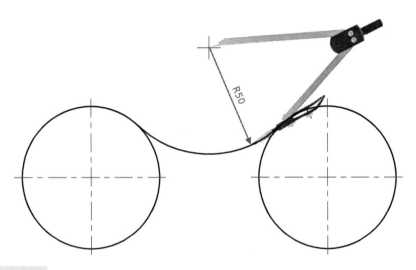

Step 4

Here the top curve is shown clearly. Notice the centre mark is displayed as a cross to show the centre of the tangent arc.

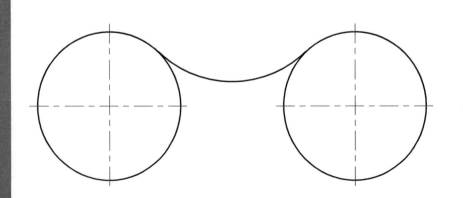

Adding the second tangent arc

Next, you need to find the centre of the other tangent arc.

As the two circles will sit inside the arc, the radii must be subtracted from one another. Therefore, the pair of compasses need to be set to:

100 – 30 = 70 mm.

An arc is drawn from the centre of one of the circles.

Step 1

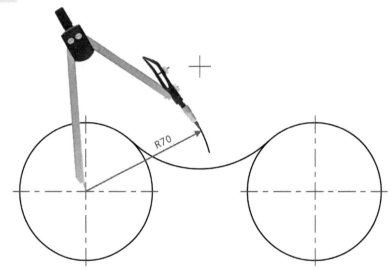

Step 2

An arc is then drawn from the centre of the other circle. The centre of the tangent arc is at the point where the two arcs intersect.

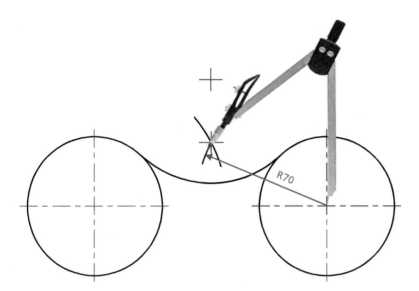

Step 3

The tangent arc can now be drawn at the correct radius.

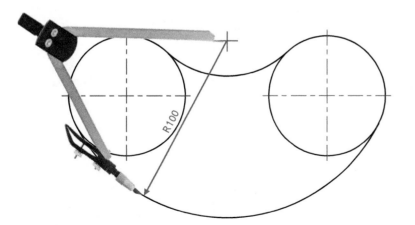

Step 4

The completed nameplate with the centre marks is shown below. Even though this method was traditionally used on a drawing board, you can use these techniques in a sketch when 3D modelling.

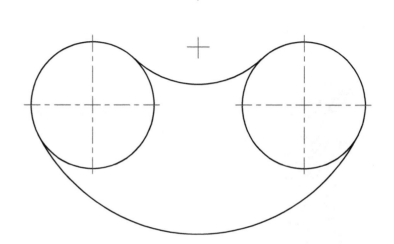

🔵 Exam Tip

It is unlikely that you will have to produce a tangency drawing in your exam. However, you must know the principles behind tangency as you could be asked to state the size of a radius used in creating a drawing.

While CAD has replaced much drawing board work, there are times when these techniques may have to be used. It is also important to understand how tangency is created.

Interpenetration of cylinders

Interpenetration is the name given to the line where two joined pipes meet.

This is shown on the illustration below.

In 3D modelling software, this is produced by using an angled workplane. However, it is important that you know how to produce a line of interpenetration using manual methods, as you may need to identify the process or select the correct view in your exam.

GO! Exam Tip

While drawing boards are not used, you can be asked to plot points on a grid, so learn this method.

Step 1

The first stage is to draw a circle on the centre line of the sloping cylinder. This needs to be done on all views.

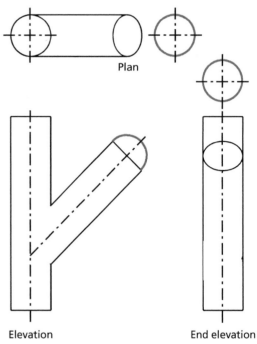

Plan

Elevation

End elevation

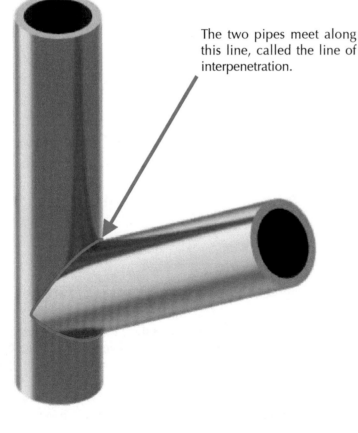

The two pipes meet along this line, called the line of interpenetration.

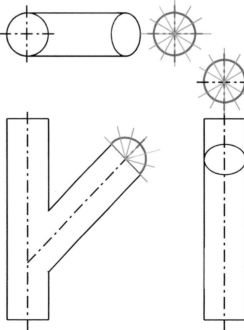

Step 2

Next, create a clock face on the circles with an angle of 30° between each line, starting from the centre line.

Step 3

Now, draw projection lines at the same angle as the pipe in each of the views.

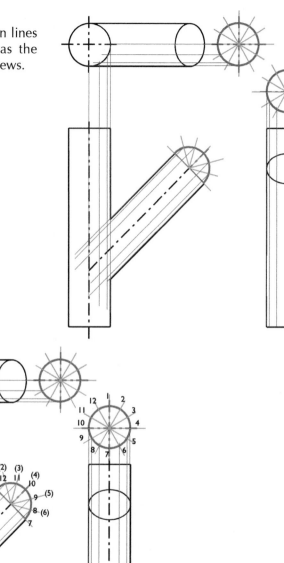

Step 4

The key stage of the process is to number the clock faces on the two views. These numbers should correspond with each other.

Step 5

The numbers enable you to find the points for the curve of interpenetration. You have to project horizontally across the views from the number 1 point to the number 1 line. Then, project from the 2 (12) point to the 2 and 12 lines, and so on.

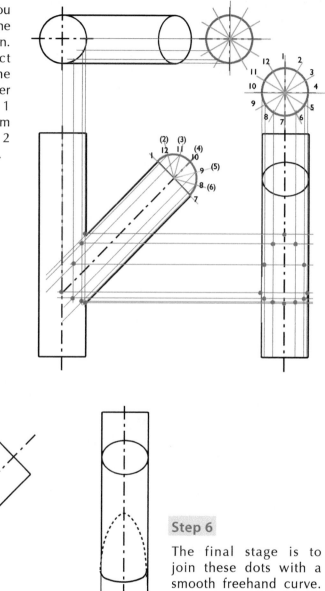

Step 6

The final stage is to join these dots with a smooth freehand curve. Remember to show hidden detail where required. This completes the line of interpenetration.

Intersections of prisms

Creating intersecting shapes is easy using modern 3D CAD packages. These software packages also generate the orthographic views of the intersecting shapes.

Old-fashioned manual methods required the draughtsperson to create these views using a projection line. It was important to accurately number each of the edges of the shapes in order to create these views.

You may be asked to demonstrate your understanding of this process in the exam.

The drawing below shows how the 45° projection line, or bounce line, can be used to generate the lengths of the edges of the prism for the elevation. Third-angle orthographic projection works on this basis to create all the parts of the views.

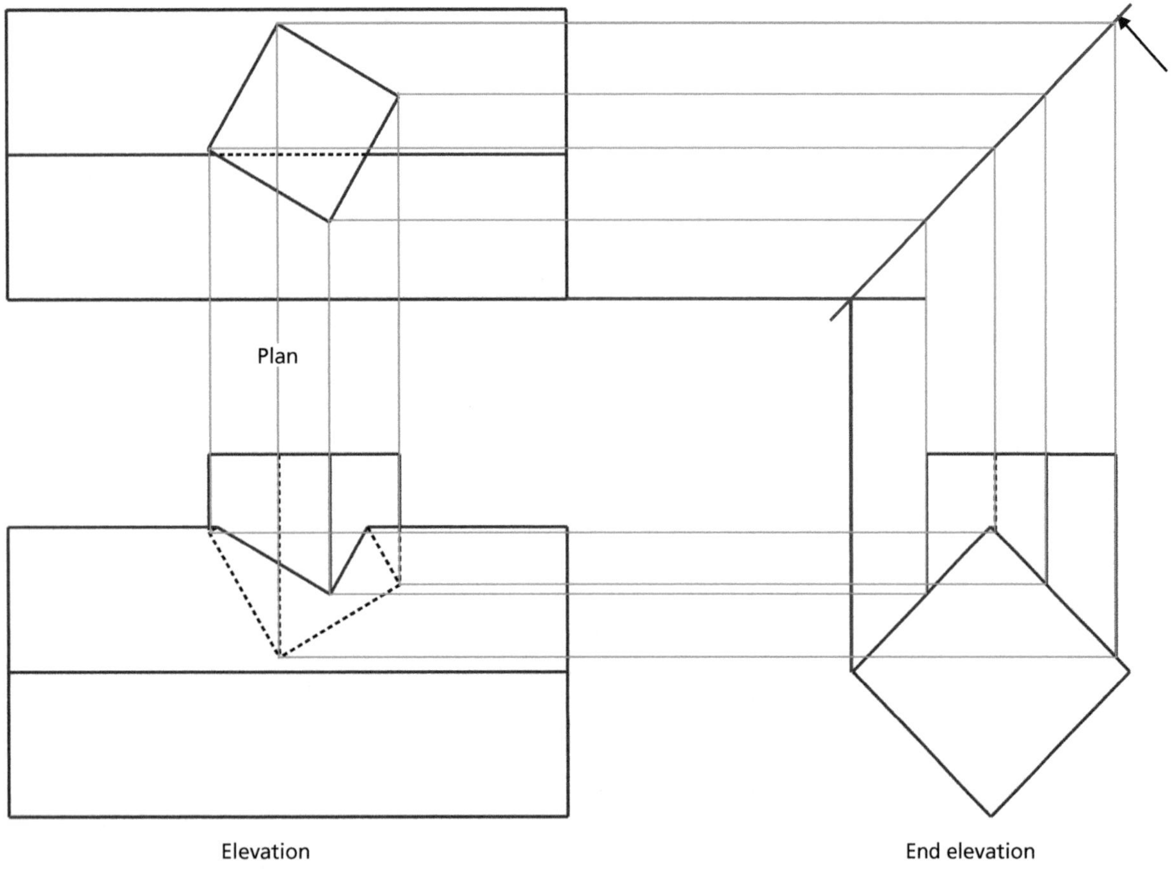

This is the 45° bounce line. The blue lines show how the start point from which it is drawn can be located.

The green lines show how the projection method enables the corners to be projected between views so that the line of intersection may be plotted.

Plan

Elevation

End elevation

GO! Exam Tip

Even though you will not be asked to draw anything in your exam, you can be asked about projection, so learn this method.

It is important to get the position of the bounce line correct. Project the bottom line of the plan horizontally and the left-hand side of the end elevation vertically. The point where the two lines (shown in dark blue) cross is where the 45° bounce line should begin.

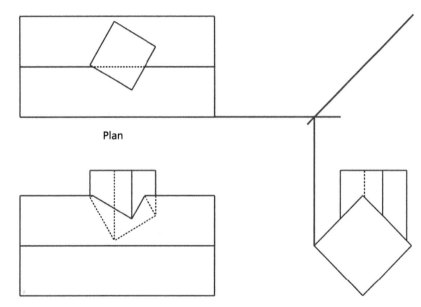

Plan

Elevation

End elevation

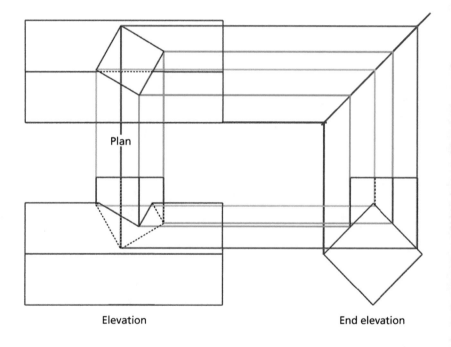

Plan

Elevation

End elevation

You can see from this diagram how the lines correspond with each other to produce the lengths of the edges of the prisms on the elevation.

True length and true shape

True length and true shape are important when talking about the sloping faces of 3D prisms. When looking at these 3D objects in an orthographic view, the viewer cannot see the actual shape of the sloping face. Viewing the face as a true shape allows this.

3D CAD packages will produce these types of views for you within an auxiliary view.

Draw horizontal lines across to the elevation from the end elevation. Make sure you draw from the top, centre and bottom of the sloping face.

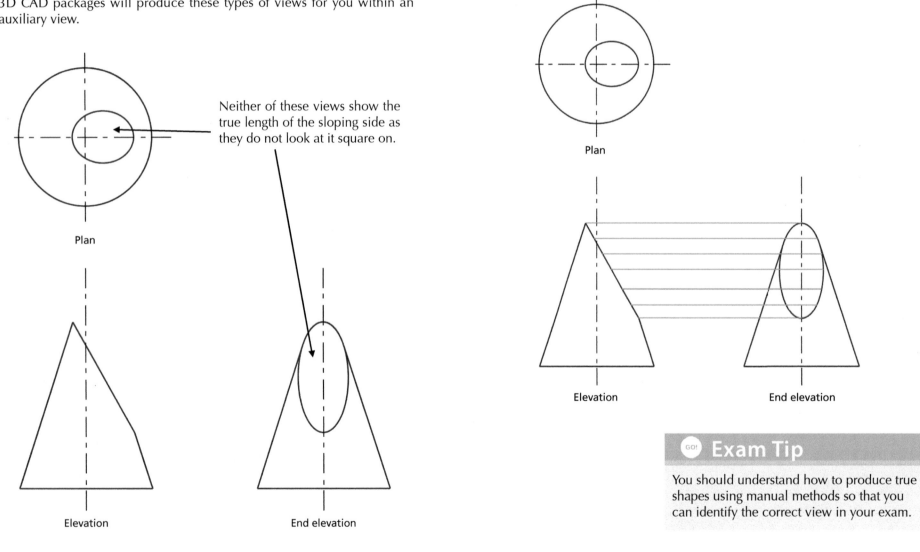

Neither of these views show the true length of the sloping side as they do not look at it square on.

Plan

Elevation

End elevation

Plan

Elevation

End elevation

Exam Tip

You should understand how to produce true shapes using manual methods so that you can identify the correct view in your exam.

Step 2

Extend the lines from the elevation at 90º to the sloping edge into the open space above the end elevation.

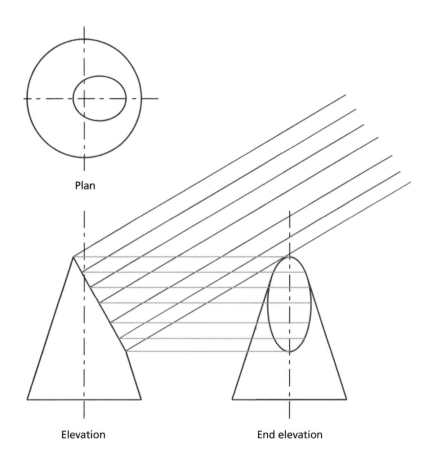

Step 3

The next step is to draw a centre line parallel to the sloping edge on the elevation in the space above the end elevation. This is important as the widths from the end elevation will be transferred onto this view from this line.

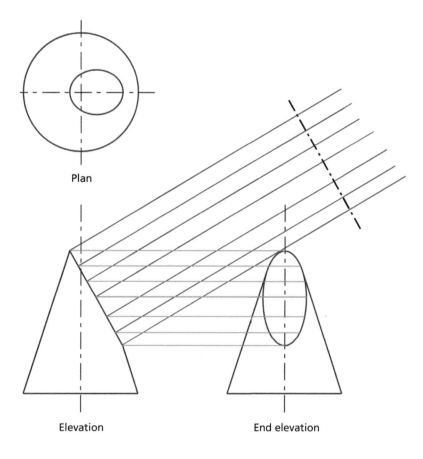

TECHNICAL DRAWINGS

Step 4

Next, use a pair of compasses to transfer the widths from the end elevation onto the true shape. Make sure you mark both sides of the centre line as shown below. Repeat this for each of the lines.

The top and bottom lines have points on the centre line.

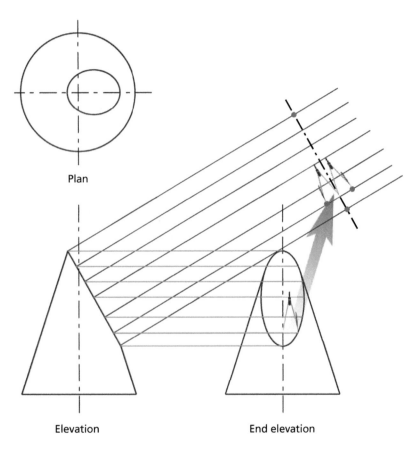

Plan

Elevation   End elevation

Step 5

To complete the drawing, draw a smooth freehand curve to join the points.

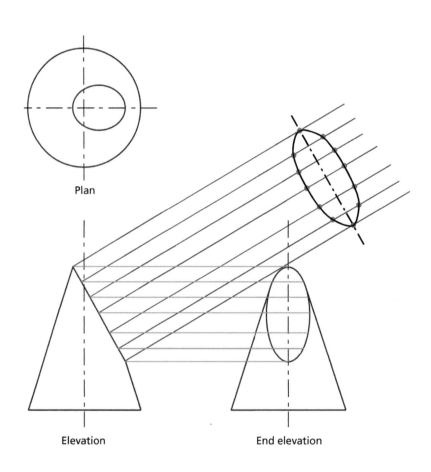

Plan

Elevation   End elevation

TECHNICAL DRAWINGS

Auxiliary views – using CAD

Auxiliary views allow true shapes to be shown in context with the rest of the view of the object.

Using 3D CAD software, auxiliary views can be created at the click of a button. However, you need to know how this is done using manual methods, as you may be asked about it in your exam.

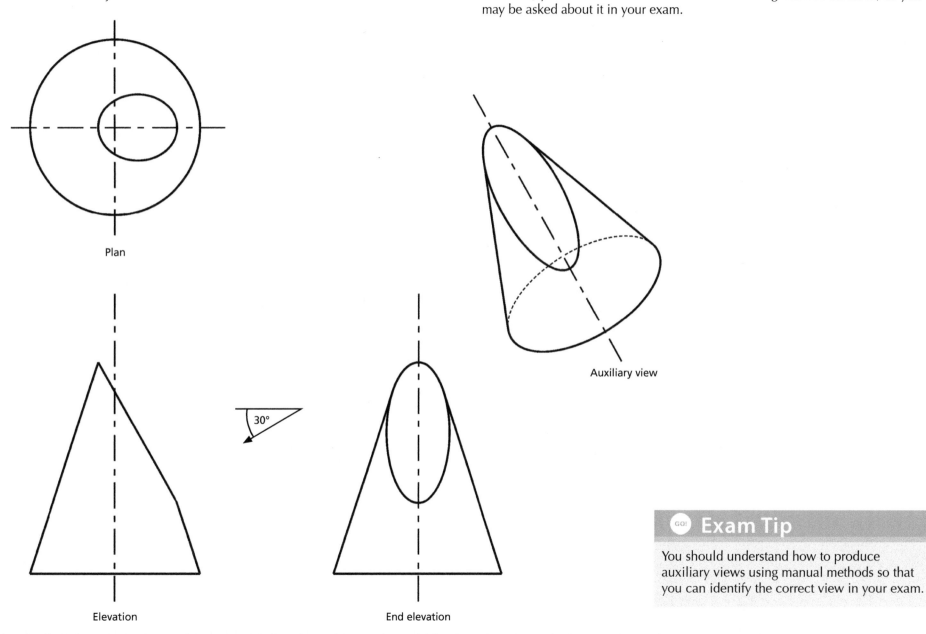

Plan

Elevation

30°

End elevation

Auxiliary view

TECHNICAL DRAWINGS

Step 1

Auxiliary views can be produced manually using the following method.
Take slices through the object and project these up to the plan.

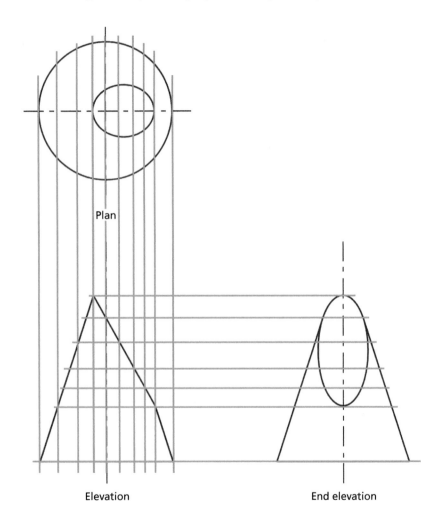

Plan

Elevation

End elevation

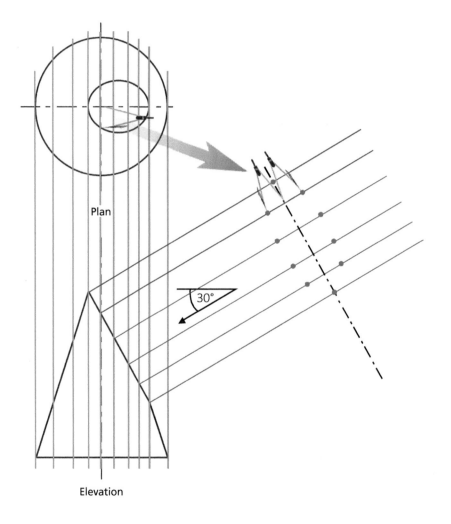

Plan

30°

Elevation

Step 2

One tip for creating auxiliary views is to complete one surface at a time. This makes it easier to keep track of the points that will be made on the drawing.

Use a pair of compasses to transfer the sizes from the next curve to the auxiliary view.

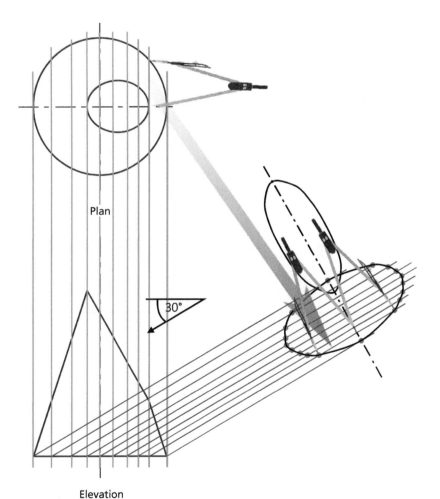

Plan

30°

Elevation

Step 3

Finally, add the outside edges to a view. Ensure that any hidden detail is shown. In this example, the part of the curve on the base needs to be shown as hidden detail.

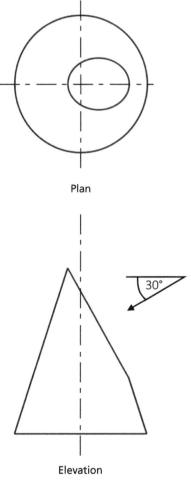

Plan

30°

Elevation

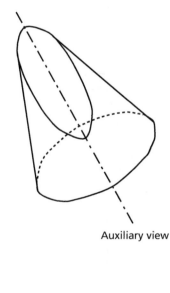

Auxiliary view

Surface development

Surface developments are flat shapes that either fold or roll to make a 3D object. This type of drawing is commonly used for manufacturing in sheet metalwork.

You can use computer software such as Pepakura Designer to produce surface developments from an STL file of a 3D model. *Please note that using the sheet metal function in Autodesk Inventor will not produce accurate drawings, so avoid using this method.*

GO! Exam Tip

You need to know how to produce surface developments using manual methods for your exam, as you may be asked to identify the correct surface development for a given view of intersecting shapes.

To produce surface developments manually, first you need to produce orthographic drawings of an object.

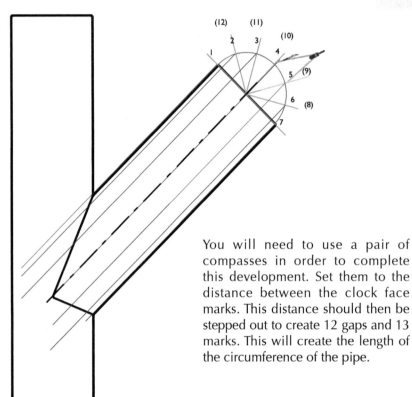

You will need to use a pair of compasses in order to complete this development. Set them to the distance between the clock face marks. This distance should then be stepped out to create 12 gaps and 13 marks. This will create the length of the circumference of the pipe.

This shows the pair of compasses being used to create the 12 spaces for the development.

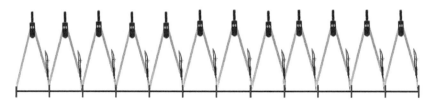

The marks should be extended upwards vertically to complete the next stage of the development.

Number the lines on the grid and use the pair of compasses to mark the lengths of the intersecting pipe onto the grid. Shown is length number 1. You should repeat this for each of the remaining lengths.

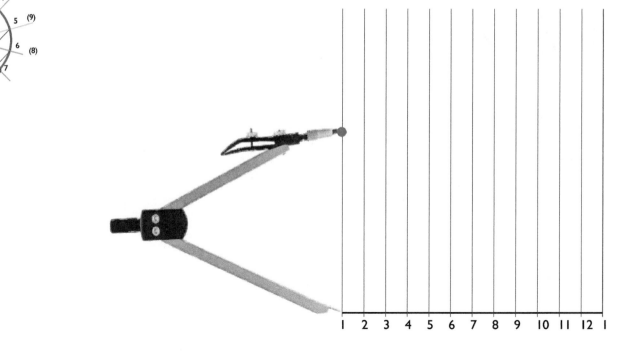

Once all of the lengths have been marked onto the development grid, you should see a pattern of marks like the one shown below.

A pair of compasses have been used to transfer all of the lengths from the elevation of the intersecting pipes onto the development.

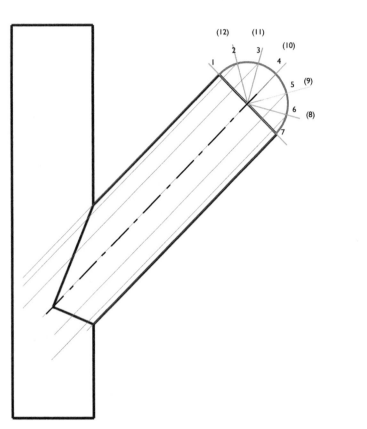

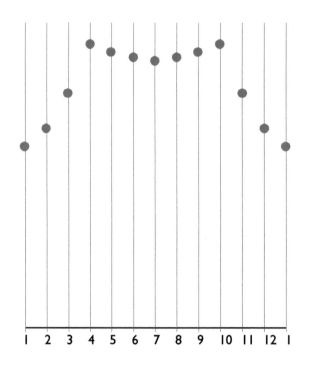

These marks should be connected using smooth, freehand curves.

Ensure that the base and outside edges are outlined to complete the development. This will make the development stand out against the construction lines.

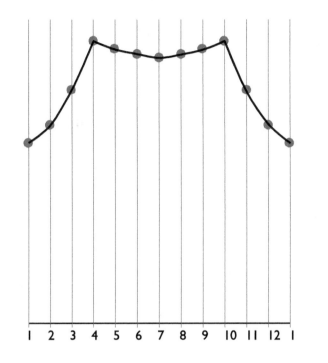

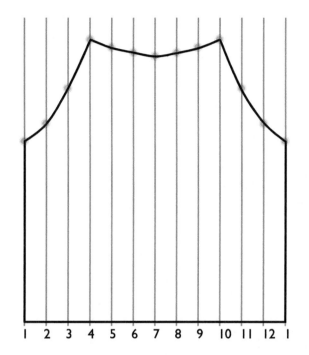

This is the manual method for creating developments of intersecting pipes. You need to have an understanding of this as you may be asked about it in the exam. You can see why it is far easier to use computer software to create these automatically from 3D CAD models and why such software is used in modern industry.

Oblique views

Oblique views are the most simplistic pictorial drawings that can be produced. An object is drawn from the front, like an elevation. The depths are then projected or sketched back at 45°. In a cabinet oblique drawing, the depths are drawn at half the full size. A cavalier oblique drawing is used when it is preferable to show the depths drawn full size.

The advantage of using oblique drawings is that circles can be shown accurately and clearly from square on and the shape of the circle is not distorted in any way. This allows engineering components to be shown clearly.

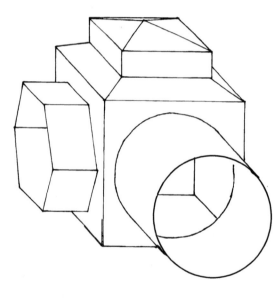

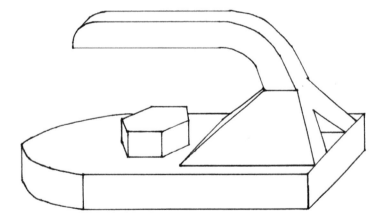

45°

 **Exam Tip**

Make sure you can identify isometric, oblique, planometric, one-point perspective and two-point perspective drawings from each other.

Planometric views

Planometric views are commonly used by interior designers. Due to the angles they are drawn at, they can clearly display the internal details of a room. Planometrics are either drawn at 45° and 45° or 30° and 60°.

Rendered CAD drawings like the one shown here are often used to show room layouts. They are produced in perspective rather than a strict planometric format to make them appear more realistic. However, their purpose (showing the interior layout of buildings) is the same.

Planometric layout

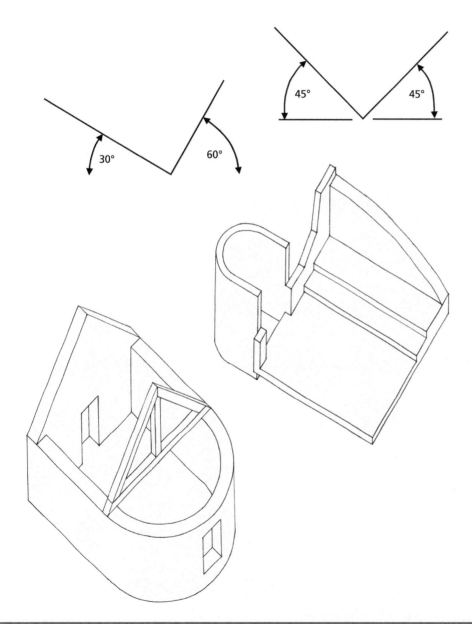

Perspective views

Perspective views are a realistic method of sketching where lengths appear to get smaller the further away from the viewer they are. Lines are taken to vanishing points in order to produce the perspective effect. You will produce one-point and two-point perspective sketches when producing preliminary drawings during the Higher Graphic Communication course. It is also likely that the CAD rendered environments you produce will be shown in perspective to give the most realistic views for promotional graphics.

Perspective layout

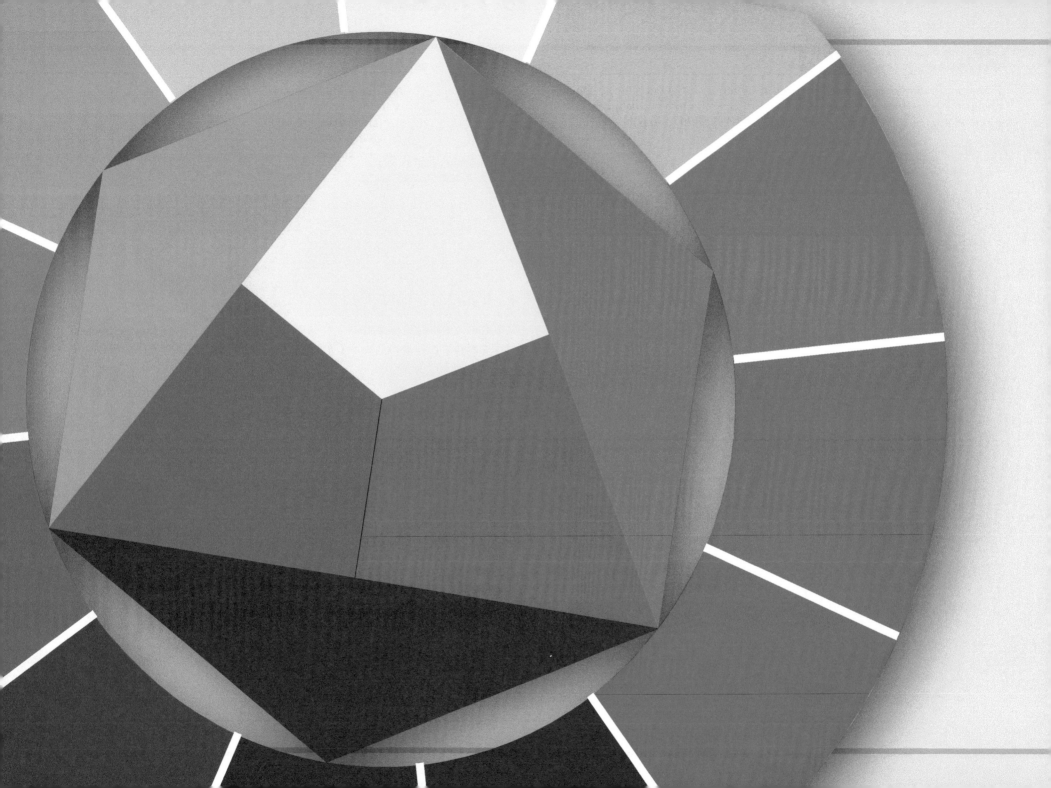

Chapter 5

Creating Promotional Layouts

You will learn

- **The colour wheel**
- **Design elements and principles**
- **Grid structure**
- **DTP features – an overview**

The colour wheel

Colour is one of the most important choices that you will make. The colour wheel is used to plan colour schemes for promotional graphics.

It quickly shows how colours will harmonise or contrast with each other.

Contrasting colours

Contrasting colours are on opposite sides of the colour wheel. They can be used together to create impact and can be eye-catching.

Harmonising colours

Harmonising colours are next to each other on the colour wheel. They can be used to create a soft or gentle feel.

Primary colours

The primary colours are red, blue and yellow.

Secondary colours

The secondary colours are violet, green and orange.

Tertiary colours

Tertiary colours are mixes of primary and secondary colours.

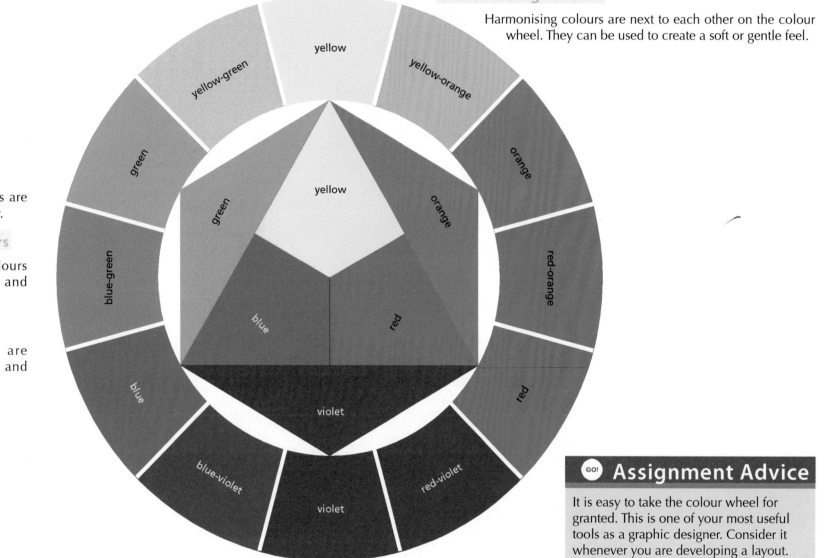

GO! Assignment Advice

It is easy to take the colour wheel for granted. This is one of your most useful tools as a graphic designer. Consider it whenever you are developing a layout.

Warm colours

Warm colours are used to give a feeling of warmth to a drawing. They can also be used to show that something is hot as part of a symbol, like a red dot on a hot water tap.

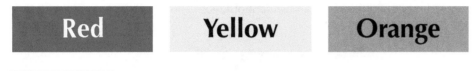

Cool colours

Cool colours are used to give a feeling of coolness to a drawing. They can also be used to show that something is cold as part of a symbol, like a blue dot on a cold water tap.

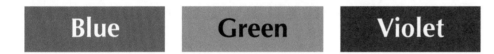

Advancing colours

Advancing colours appear to come towards you when you look at them. They are often used to create impact.

Advancing colours tend to be warm colours:

Receding colours

Receding colours appear to move into the background when you look at them. They are often used as flashbars as they will make an object placed on top of them appear to come forward.

Receding colours tend to be cool colours:

Accent colours

An accent colour is a colour used throughout a presentation to help bring it all together. A common mistake is to use too many colours in a presentation. Using one or two colours repeatedly can help to bring all the elements together and create unity.

It's more than just music

GO! Assignment Advice

When you are evaluating the various versions of your planned layout during your assignment, refer to the headings relating to colour theory. This will help to meet the assessment requirements for DTP development work.

Design elements and principles

When planning layouts for promotional graphics, there are some guidelines to follow to help produce high-quality presentations.

These can be split into two groups:

- design elements
- design principles.

Design elements

- line
- shape
- texture
- size
- colour
- mass/weight

Design principles

- alignment
- balance
- contrast
- depth
- dominance
- unity
- proximity
- white space
- proportion
- rhythm
- emphasis
- value
- grid structure

By using these elements and principles and applying them with skill, you can create exciting and impactful presentations for your promotional graphics.

> **GO! Exam Tip**
>
> List the design elements and principles in the extra space at the end of your exam paper as soon as you begin. There will be a question about them and referring to each of them in turn will help you to write your answer.

Line

You can use line to create many different effects. Some common uses of line include organising parts of a layout, separating parts of a layout or suggesting movement within a layout.

Line can be changed by using different types, styles and colours. Curved or wavy lines can be used to suggest movement or create interest.

The cover of the dice design project shown below uses line to underline text, separate the text on the page from images, act as a flashbar to bring images forward and act as a visual border for the cover. The curved lines create movement through the different dice shown and help bring them forwards towards the reader.

Shape

There are lots of shapes used in presentations. Commonly, these will include squares, circles, triangles and polygons like hexagons or octagons.

Squares and rectangles surround us in life so tend to be trusted. They can be seen as boring, but can be made more interesting by rotating them and placing them on top of each other.

Circles and ellipses are used to show a number of different feelings. They are protective, as they suggest a safe region, and they can also be used to suggest movement. As these shapes have no beginning or end point, they can be used to infer reliability and are often used in symbols for car manufacturers for this reason.

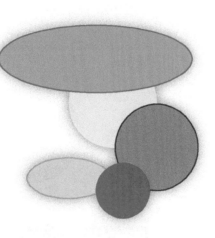

Triangles tend to suggest movement. They can be used to communicate conflict in a presentation due to their sharp corners. They can also be used to show strength and create impact.

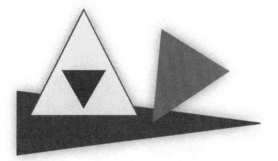

Texture

Texture affects the physical feel of the paper used. In product brochures, high-quality paper is used to imply that the product is high quality too.

Texture can also be created by the images on the paper. Old paper can be mimicked using images. Other materials can be represented through the fill options in your DTP software.

Size

Size can be used in a number of ways. When designing a presentation, you must consider the size of the paper used and how you use the size of fonts and images to highlight the most important elements of the presentation.

Larger objects will be the first things that people notice about your presentation.

Colour

The colour palette is the most important decision to make when designing a DTP layout. You must consider which colours to use based on a number of different factors.

These will include the company colours, and whether or not you want to convey emotion, present information or appeal to a particular market.

Primary colours can be used together to create contrast and target a product or presentation at a particular audience, such as young children.

Warm colours

Yellow, orange and red are considered warm colours and can create a feeling of aggression, excitement or danger. These colours appear to advance from the page.

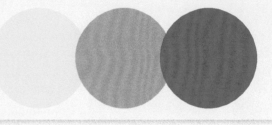

Cool colours

Blue, green and violet are cool, calming colours. They are also receding colours and can be used for flashbars, to help an object stand out from the page.

Neutral colours

Brown, black, white and grey are neutral colours and can be used to create formal, natural or simple presentations.

Mass/weight

Mass refers to the size of an element or the amount of space it occupies. The mass of an object can be increased by giving it dark colours or by making it larger in size.

When choosing text styles, their mass and weight should be considered. Chunky fonts will add mass to an area of the presentation, while smaller-structured fonts can be used to help balance a promotional item.

Mass and weight are commonly used in relation to other items on the page to create rhythm.

Alignment

There are five main types of alignment:

1. Top alignment

2. Bottom alignment

3. Left alignment

4. Right alignment

5. Centre alignment
(horizontal or/and vertical).

Alignment is often used to add structure to a DTP layout so that it is easier to follow and looks visually organised. Effective use of alignment will help the reader to follow a DTP layout as it was intended to be read. Alignment can create a visual connection between various elements of the layout, which makes it clear that these elements (e.g. text and an image) are linked.

Balance

Balance can be radial, symmetrical or asymmetrical. This is like thinking of the page as a set of scales. A heavy object can be balanced by smaller objects positioned further away from it and lighter objects can be balanced by darker objects (darker objects appear to have more weight than lighter ones).

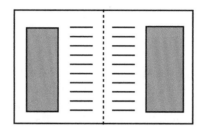

Contrast

Contrast is where opposites are used in some design features for effect. This could be shape, text, colour, line or weight.

A word in a *contrasting font*, colour or SIZE makes it **stand out**.

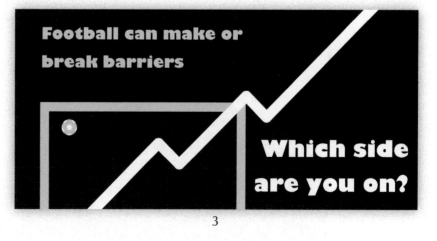

Depth

A presentation can be given a sense of depth by arranging the elements in front or behind each other. This can make some parts of the DTP presentation appear to come towards the viewer.

In the example below, the object being advertised is placed in front of both a wavy line and a gradient fill flashbar. This combination of DTP features makes the image appear to come forward. This effect is further enhanced by the use of a drop shadow.

Dominance

Dominance refers to how you can make particular parts of the presentation stand out. Dominance is all about size. The largest items on a page are the most dominant features. It means that the presentation is read in a particular order due to the relative size of the elements within it. This is known as the hierarchy of the layout.

In the example below, the product being advertised is the most dominant element, then the woman wearing headphones and then, finally, the text describing the product. Visually directing the order, or hierarchy, in which the poster is read helps the viewer to quickly understand what the product is.

Unity

Unity can be created in a presentation through repetition of shape, use of images with a common theme, repetition of font styles and the positioning of different parts in relation to one another. Overlapping elements on a layout can create unity as this develops a physical connection between elements.

The advertisement below uses red and white throughout to make it clear that all the elements belong together. The repetition of curves in the lines and subheading also creates unity. The image of the headphones tidy and the image of the woman overlap the waves in the background, which also creates unity through a physical connection.

Proximity

Proximity refers to how close together two items are positioned in a layout. The closer together the elements of a layout, the more obvious it is that they belong together. So, images could be positioned close to or overlapping each other or images and text could be placed in close proximity. When text is to be close to an image, text wrap is often used to keep it as close to the image as possible.

White space

White space is the areas on a page that are left blank. This can be used to help balance a presentation or to focus the reader's attention on the content of the presentation. White space is vitally important to prevent a presentation from being too busy or cluttered.

The blank areas on the advertisement below ensure that the viewer focuses on the images and text without any distractions.

Proportion

Proportion is all about the relationship between elements in a presentation. Large images will dominate a layout and can communicate to the readers what it is about before they even start to read the text.

On the advertisement on page 90, the images account for half the area of the advert. This effective use of proportion graphically emphasises the topic of the advert. The title is clear and helps to link the two images.

Grid structures can help you to incorporate proportion. When designing a grid structure for a longer publication, like a magazine or a book, it can be good to use different proportions on either side of a spread (two facing pages). This prevents the pages from looking too boring or regimented. You can see how the left and right margins of the facing pages in the master page for this book are reversed in order to give better proportions across the two-page spread. This also helps to create a nice rhythm, as the reader is guided from the outside to the centre of the book.

Larger margin on the outside of the page than inside for good proportions.

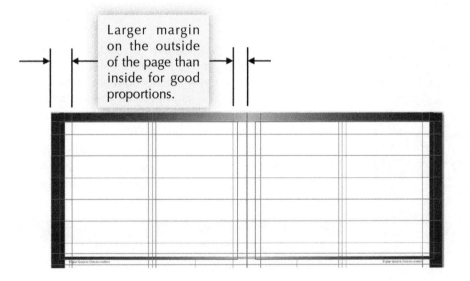

Rhythm

Rhythm is used to create movement through a presentation. This can be achieved by repeating elements and using shapes to infer movement. Various parts of a presentation can be connected with lines, shapes or colours.

The use of triangles here gives the business card rhythm by creating movement from the top left corner to the bottom right corner. The repeated use of golf balls also creates rhythm by leading the reader along the top and bottom of the card toward the contact details.

Emphasis

You can place emphasis on particular parts of a presentation by using various techniques. Bold text can be used to make particular words or parts of a presentation stand out. Text along a path can be used to contrast with other more regular shapes in a presentation. Drop shadows can give emphasis to both images and text. Bold and reverse text can also be used to make a particular feature stand out from the presentation.

Some features of a presentation can be used as a focal point in order to attract attention and quickly convey the subject of the presentation.

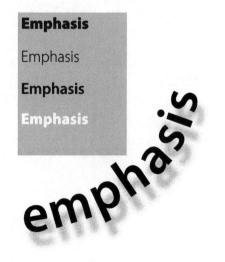

Value

Value relates to how dark or light a colour appears on a layout. It also applies to white if you use a coloured background. Value can be used to create varying amounts of contrast. In this example, the first letter 'a' has a white value of 10%, the second has a white value of 50% while the third has a value of 100%. The background also has a value of 100%, but this time in black. You can see that the bigger the difference in value between the letters and the background, the more contrast is created. Smaller differences in value are used for more subtle layouts, while greater differences in value can be used for more eye-catching layouts. Repeated shapes with increasing value can create movement or rhythm to guide the reader's eye across the page.

Grid structure

Rule of thirds

The rule of thirds is a guide used by photographers that is inspired by the golden ratio. Imagine a grid that splits a page into three equal segments both horizontally and vertically and place the main parts of your presentation on these grid lines. Some cameras have this function installed on them to assist with layout.

Here is a picture of the V&A design museum in Dundee. You can see how the main features (the sign, the opening and the window) have been split up into this rule of thirds grid to help the balance of the picture.

GO! Assignment Advice

When you evaluate the planned layout for your assignment, ensure that you use the terms covered in this section in your annotations. You need to comment on the role they play in your DTP presentation to meet the assessment requirements.

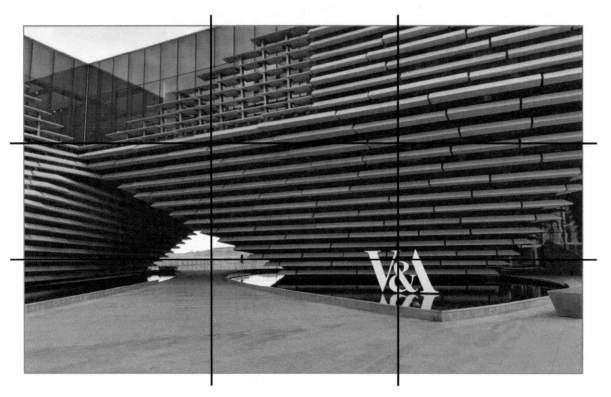

The rule of thirds can be used as a basis for grid structures to help lay out DTP presentations or to inform asymmetrical grid structures.

Symmetrical grid structure

Symmetrical grid structures are the same on both sides of a layout. They are formal and used when order is important and the layout needs to be highly organised.

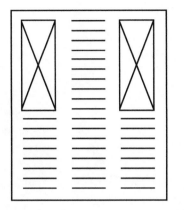

Asymmetrical grid structure

In an asymmetrical grid structure, the two sides of a page or double-page spread are different. Using this type of grid structure can create impact and interest and make something look modern or appeal to young people.

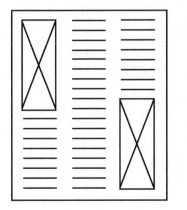
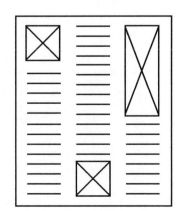

Choosing a grid

Often, designers will explore different methods of structuring a layout by quickly sketching some ideas. However, the majority of the development of the layout will be completed using DTP software. This gives the advantage of being able to use real images, the various DTP features and the quality of production that using computer software offers over hand-produced methods. It also speeds up the development process.

You can see how the designer has developed the structure of the layouts below using DTP software. Each has been developed through stages using images and all of the DTP features.

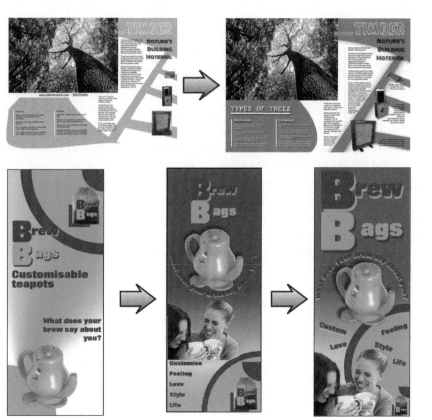

DTP features – an overview

Look at the layout on the right. We will describe how the design elements and design principles have been used to produce this layout.

Proportion – The image is the largest element on the page. The reader will notice this first, so it creates a hierarchy in the layout. The title is the next thing to be noticed, as it is the second largest item, which leads the reader to the main part of the magazine article.

Line – This is used to help organise the text at the bottom left-hand side of the layout. The lines guide the reader down the columns of text containing the examples of types of tree.

Line is also used as a column rule to help separate the columns of text on the facing page, so it is easier to read.

Balance – The mass of the left-hand side of the page helps to balance the busy right-hand side of the page where most of the information in the article is located.

Alignment – The text 'Types of Trees' is left aligned with the line that the hardwoods are listed alongside.

The text on the far right-hand side of the page is all right aligned to create structure and a clear relationship between all of the elements.

Texture – The texture of the tree bark and leaves in the image contrasts with the smooth background underneath the image, which has been used to make the text stand out from the image and easier to read.

Size – The ever-decreasing sizes of text direct the reader from the main heading to the subheadings and then on to the extended body text.

TYPES OF TREES

Hardwoods

Beech – a very hard, straight-grained wood, which can survive in harsh conditions.

Mahogany – a reddish-brown wood often used to make expensive furniture.

Oak – a very hard wood, which requires a high level of skill when working with it.

Teak – this wood is highly resistant to outdoor conditions, making it ideal for garden furniture.

Softwoods

Scots pine – this wood contains lots of knots, but is easy to work with.

Spruce – although not particularly durable, this wood is often used for fence panelling.

Yellow cedar – this is a pale yellow, light wood, which can be quite stable.

European redwood – this is a cheap wood with lots of knots. However, once a protective finish is applied it is quite durable.

TIMBER

Nature's Building Material

testing weather elements and appear natural in parks.

Furniture and smaller decorative pieces have been produced for centuries by the people of the time. School pupils have designed and made an impressive range of wooden items over the decades where Woodworking has been taught.

These have ranged from smaller pieces to introduce pupils to tools and techniques to more complex pieces of furniture to showcase their talents.

Some of these projects allow a traditional material to meet the requirements of objects of the modern world. Beautiful amplifiers that will allow music to be played from a phone and keyrings that double as a stand while watching TV shows or movies online are two examples of schools projects that are created by pupils in Technical departments in the UK.

Trees are not only the lungs of our planet but also supply a strong and beautiful material.

Hardwoods lose their leaves in winter while softwoods are evergreen. Not all hardwoods are hard like their name suggests. Balsa is one example of this where it is a light and soft wood often used for making model aircraft.

Wood is also often used for building childrens' play areas as it will stand up to

Smaller items can be created from wood.

A traditional material like wood can be used to make modern pieces like the amplifier shown. The contrast of technology and natural materials can create a simple yet dramatic effect.

Frames can be built from wood. These can be free standing, double sided like the one pictured or, more commonly, can be hung on walls.

Colour – Green is used throughout the layout to reinforce that trees are a natural resource.

Rhythm – The repeated squares leading into the heading 'Timber' lead the reader from the large image to the main article.

Shape – The green, sloping shape is used to direct the reader down the page, through the various parts of the layout. The branches off the main shape reflect the structure of a tree, reinforcing the topic of the article.

Emphasis – Drop shadows have been added to the titles on the left page, the images of the products and the background shapes to make them stand out from the page.

Proximity – The images of the products are positioned close to the descriptions to make it obvious that they belong together.

Contrast – The heading and subheading contrast so that they can be easily distinguished from each other. This makes the different parts of the article easier to read.

The images are placed on green shapes that act as flashbars to help them stand out. Additionally, the drop shadows on both the shapes and images help them to stand out from the background.

White space – There is some white space between the main image and the column of text to create some breathing room (an area where the reader's eye isn't distracted by lots of information). There is also space between the images of the wooden products, which creates an invisible boundary between each of them.

Unity – Green is used throughout the article to help bring all the elements together.

GO! Exam Tip

You will be asked to describe how the design elements and design principles have been used to create an effective promotional graphic. State the design element or design principle you are describing first, then explain how it has been used in the presentation.

Chapter 6

3D CAD Modelling

You will learn

- 2D CAD drawing tools
- 3D CAD features and edits
- Using a revolve
- Using the loft tool
- Extrude/sweep along a path
- Using a swept blend
- Types of helix
- Creating a helix
- Intersecting features
- Applying a shell
- Applying a fillet to an edge

- Applying a chamfer to an edge
- The mirror edit
- Using the array tool
- 2D CAD constraints
- Assembling parts of a model
- Offset
- Tangency
- Assembly files
- Sub-assembly
- Stock or library components – CAD libraries

- 3D CAD views
- 3D CAD rendering techniques
- Terms involved in 3D modelling
- Modelling concepts
- Modelling tree/hierarchy
- Modelling plan
- CAD file types
- CAD libraries
- Online CAD libraries

2D CAD drawing tools

When creating 3D CAD models, you have to use sketches (2D drawings made in the software, from which the models are created). To do this, you will need to use the drawing tools within the software to produce different shapes. Some of these 2D drawing tools are similar to those used in programs like Word, so it is likely that you will be familiar with them already.

Line tool

The line tool allows straight lines to be drawn.

Circle tool

The circle tool allows you to produce circles.

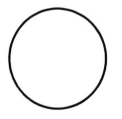

Rectangle tool

The rectangle tool allows rectangles or squares to be drawn.

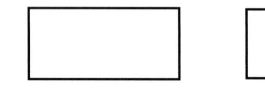

Ellipse tool

Ellipses can be drawn using the ellipse tool.

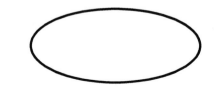

Trim tool

Unnecessary lines can be removed from a sketch. These lines may have been included to assist with creating the sketch, but can be removed once their use has passed.

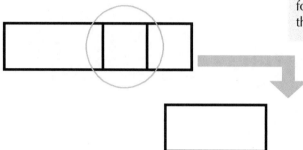

Mirror tool

The mirror tool allows the user to create a mirror image of a shape.

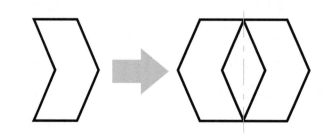

Layers in CAD

When using layers in CAD, it is similar to drawing the different details of a drawing on tracing paper. You can draw different details of a drawing on separate sheets within the CAD package. These sheets are called layers. They can be viewed independently or together depending on what the person reading the drawings needs to see. For example, the electrical wiring can be drawn on one layer and viewed separately from the plumbing fittings, which can be drawn on a different layer.

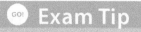 **Exam Tip**

Quote these terms when describing how you would produce a sketch for a 3D CAD model in the modelling questions.

Arrays (linear, box and radial)

The array tool allows you to repeat the same shape in a pattern. This saves time, as you do not need to redraw shapes. A linear array repeats the shape in a straight line, a box array repeats it in two directions and a radial array repeats it in a circular pattern.

Linear array

Box array

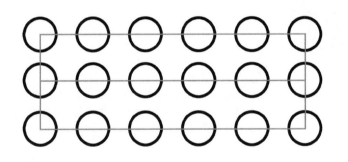

Radial array

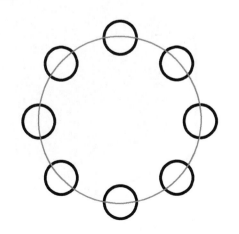

Offset tool

The offset tool will create a line, curve or shape a specified distance from another line or the edge of a shape.

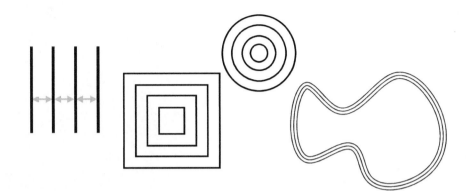

Project edge tool

The project edge function allows you to take a length, or chain of lengths, from a solid and copy (or project) it onto the sketch. This is very useful when it is important to repeat the lengths from a solid on a sketch. This tool is often used in top-down modelling (see page 134).

The outside edges of the solid on the left are repeated on the sketch here.

Extend tool

Lines can be extended from sketches to meet the beginning of another sketch. Here, the line is extended across to close the gap in the shape.

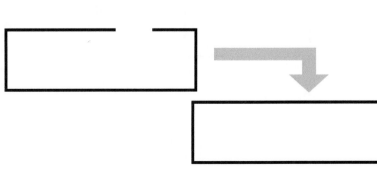

3D CAD features and edits

Creating an extrusion

Extrusions are the backbone of most 3D CAD models. They are the most simple CAD feature available. They create a solid by dragging a shape along a straight line, either up or down, right or left, or forward or back.

The die shown here was created using a number of different extrusions.

You can do three things when extruding shapes:

1. Add material to create solid objects.

2. Subtract material from solid objects.

3. Intersect other solids.

Step 1

To create a cube, like the die shown, a profile of a square needs to be drawn as a sketch.

The sketch of the square will look like this.

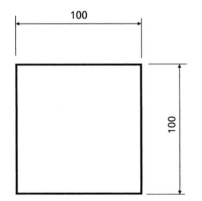

Exam Tip

When describing an extrusion, use the following terms:

Step 1: Sketch a **profile** showing the correct dimensions.

Step 2: **Extrude** to a distance.

Use the term **subtract** if removing material from a solid. Show the dimensions used for the profile using sketches. This will make it easier to understand than describing this using words.

Exam Tip

Use sketches to illustrate your description of the 3D CAD modelling process. This will help you achieve full marks. Show the profiles and dimensions of the lines using sketches. Do not attempt to describe the sketch required for a profile through words alone. The quality and proportions of these sketches do not matter.

Step 2

The square is then extruded to create a solid shape. In this case, the extrude was set to the size required to make a cube.

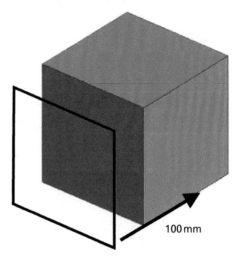

100mm

Subtracting a solid/features

When you remove material from a solid, you must describe this as a subtraction. The numbers on the die are all subtracted from the solid. This is done using the extrude tool with the subtract setting switched on.

Extrude, revolve, extrude along a path, loft and helix can all be used to create a solid and can be switched to subtract from a solid model.

This 3D CAD model of a desk tidy has been created using only extrusions. You should use the extrude feature whenever a 2D shape can be stretched in a straight line, to a given length, in order to add or subtract material.

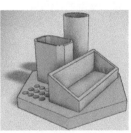

The extrusion feature has also been used to create all of the components within the TV units seen below. With all of them, a 2D shape has been created then pulled out in a straight line. Either of these two types of 3D CAD models could be used in promotional graphics.

A solid CAD model, rendered showing materials, shadows, reflections and perspective.

A solid CAD model with an artistic view applied. This shows perspective, shadows and form.

The circular profile for the dot is sketched first.

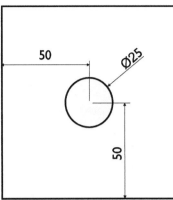

50

Ø25

50

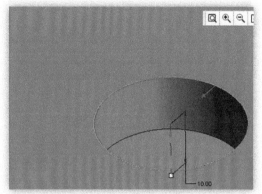

The depth of the extrusion must be specified.

You must also state that you are subtracting material.

Once completed, it will look like this.

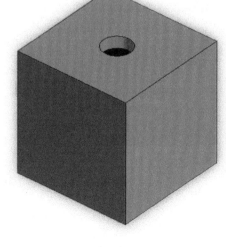

Using a revolve

The revolve feature allows a sketch to be rotated around a centre axis and a solid shape to be created from this. A shape must have rotational symmetry for a revolve to be suitable.

The first stage is to create a sketch with a centre line. The centre line is the centre axis for the revolve. It is important to position the sketch at the correct distance from the centre line for the revolve to be created to the correct dimensions.

Step 1

The profile of the revolve

The profile is the cross section of the revolve. This is the part that is rotated around the centre axis to form the solid.

Step 2

Position of the centre axis

The centre axis for the revolve is shown here. A centre axis is drawn as a centre line in a sketch. In this example, the gap between the sketch and the centre line will mean that there is a hollow part in the middle of the revolve.

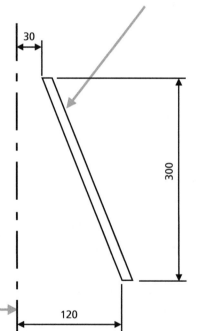

Step 3

Creating the solid

The solid that is created from the sketch is shown here. You can see the revolve was taken around a full 360° and the profile is highlighted in green.

The revolve angle

In this revolve, the profile was taken around 360°.

The profile

The profile is shown in green.

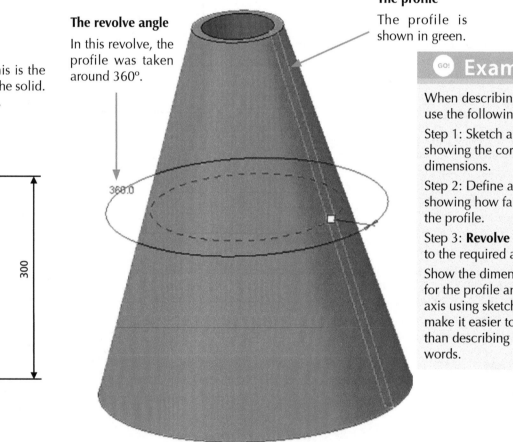

GO! Exam Tip

When describing a revolve, use the following terms:

Step 1: Sketch a **profile** showing the correct dimensions.

Step 2: Define a **centre axis**, showing how far it is from the profile.

Step 3: **Revolve** the profile to the required angle.

Show the dimensions used for the profile and centre axis using sketches. This will make it easier to understand than describing this using words.

3D CAD MODELLING

The revolve tool

The revolve tool can be used to create many different shapes. Just remember that the solid must have rotational symmetry.

It is likely that the solid created when using the revolve tool will have a circular shape to it. This is one way of deciding whether or not this is the most suitable modelling tool to use.

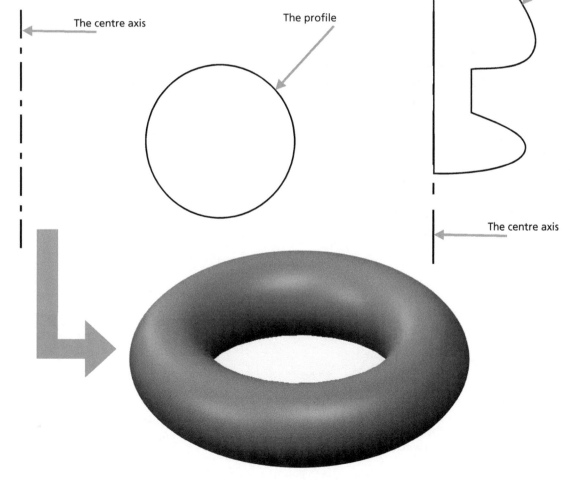

The centre axis

The profile

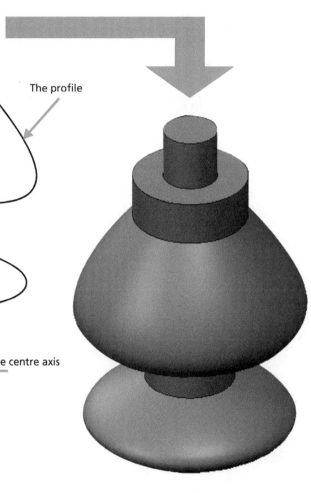

The profile

The centre axis

Exam Tip

The position of the centre axis relative to the profile is very important when producing a revolve, so make sure you define this clearly in your modelling plan.

Using the loft tool

The loft feature allows a range of shapes with different cross sections to be joined together. This can be done with the sections sketched on parallel planes, like the example shown here, or along a path.

Some 3D modelling packages refer to a loft as a 'blend' and approach the command differently. However, it is very important that you refer to this command as a loft in the exam and follow the process for a loft in your answer. It is the only answer or description that will be accepted by the SQA in an exam as correct.

An example of a solid created through lofting is shown here. The three sketches that have been used to create the loft are highlighted in pink in the solid.

Step 1

Creating workplanes

To begin, you must create workplanes for each of the profiles of the loft.

In this case, three workplanes need to be created with the required distance between them. In 3D CAD packages, these workplanes are known as offset workplanes.

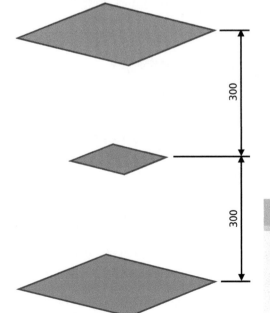

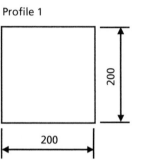

Profile 3

Profile 2

Profile 1

Step 2

Sketching the profiles

The three profiles now need to be sketched. You must show the dimensions used for these profiles.

Previous sketches are shown lighter in Profile 2 and Profile 3 for clarity. You need to show where any new sketch is positioned relative to previous sketches.

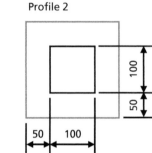

Profile 1

Profile 2

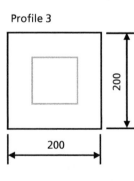

Profile 3

GO1

Exam Tip

You must use the term **loft** in your exam to describe this feature. Any other commands used by software packages that describe the same process will not be accepted as correct answers.

Step 3

Creating the solid

Now use the loft tool and select the three sketches to create the solid. Define the loft path as straight.

Creating a loft path for a twist

If a loft has a twist in it, like the one shown here, you need to define a path that the loft should follow.

You can show this path by drawing a line from one of the corners of each of the three sketches.

You must clearly show the path that a loft follows in a modelling plan and in any exam answers you give.

The path is shown in green in the image on the right. You can see how the path moves along one corner at a time as it moves up through the three profiles.

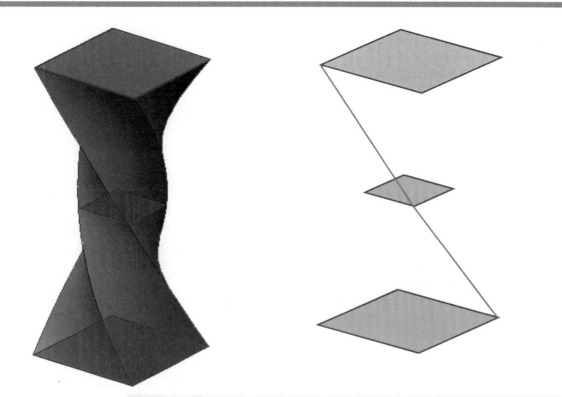

🟢 GO! Exam Tip

When describing a loft, use the following terms:

Step 1: Create **workplanes** showing the dimensions between each.

Step 2: Sketch **profiles of each** slice of the loft showing all the dimensions and making it clear which workplane they are on.

Step 3: Define a **loft path**.

Step 4: Use the **loft** feature to create the loft.

Show the dimensions used for the workplanes and profile using sketches. This will make it easier to understand than describing this using words.

🟢 GO! Exam Tip

Practising sketching workplanes like this and including the dimensions will help your exam performance.

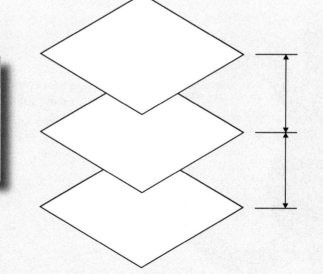

3D CAD MODELLING

Extrude/sweep along a path

The extrude along a path (or sweep along a path) tool allows the user to form a solid along a sketched path. Either term (extrude along a path or sweep along a path) is acceptable in the exam.

The teapot handle shown here was created by extruding along a path.

Step 1

The profile of the extrude needs to be sketched.

Step 2

The path the extrude along a path will follow must be sketched.

Step 3

The extrude tool can then be used to create the solid.

The solid shown in yellow was created by the profile following the path.

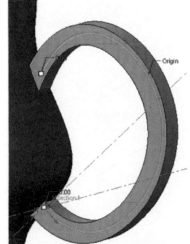

Some 3D CAD software packages ask the user to select the workplanes for the profile and the path manually. If you have to do this, ensure that these workplanes are perpendicular to one another.

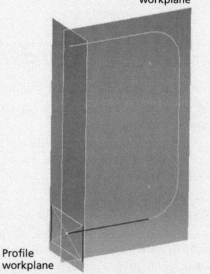

Using a swept blend

A swept blend is a combination of lofting and extrusion along a path. It allows the solid to have different cross sections along the path, as shown here in the teapot spout.

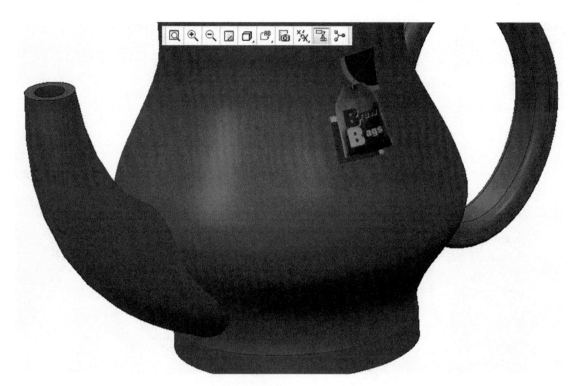

The teapot spout is created by first sketching a path, then sketching a cross section at one end of the path and a second, different cross section at the other end of the path.

The small circle at the top of the spout is the first section of the swept blend.

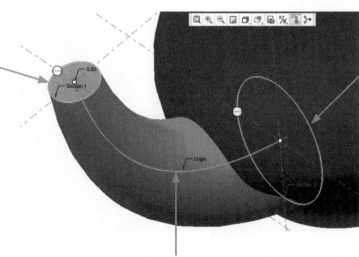

The large circle at the base of the teapot is the second section of the swept blend.

The path of the swept blend is shown here.

GO! **Exam Tip**

This command will not be included in your Higher exam. It has only been included in this guide to help you with more advanced coursework.

3D CAD MODELLING

Types of helix

A helix is a spring-like solid. It can have a regular path or angled path. It can also follow a constant pitch or a varied pitch.

The pitch is the distance between each of the points on the curve.

Examples of helix are shown here.

A helix can be created with a taper. This can be done by changing the taper angle.

Pen springs often have a varied pitch. This can be modelled using a helix and changing the settings to allow this.

Car springs tend to be larger in size and are more likely to use a constant pitch.

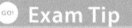

Exam Tip

When describing a helix, use the following terms:

Step 1: Sketch a **centre axis**.

Step 2: Sketch a **profile** showing all dimensions and the distance from the centre axis.

Step 3: Define the **pitch**.

Step 4: Define the **direction** (clockwise or anticlockwise).

Step 5: Define the **length** of the helix or the **number of turns** in it.

Step 6: Create the **Helix**.

Show the dimensions used for the profile, centre axis and offset distance using sketches. This will make it easier to understand than describing this using words.

Creating a helix

You must follow these steps when creating a helix:

1. Sketch the centre axis for the helix.

2. Create the profile of the helix.

3. Set the size of the pitch. (This is the distance between the points on the individual coils of the helix.)

4. Define whether the helix is clockwise or anticlockwise.

5. Define the length of the helix or the number of revolutions you would like it to have.

Steps 1 and 2

Create the centre axis and the profile for the helix. The centre axis will be defined as a centre line in the sketch. The profile will be a closed shape. You must define the dimensions of the profile and its distance from the centre axis (the offset distance).

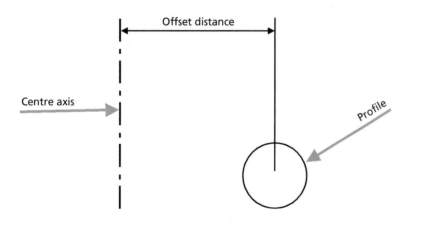

Step 3

Set the pitch of the helix. The pitch is the distance between the individual turns. The pitch cannot be made smaller than the height of the profile.

The pitch is the distance between the points on the individual coils of the helix.

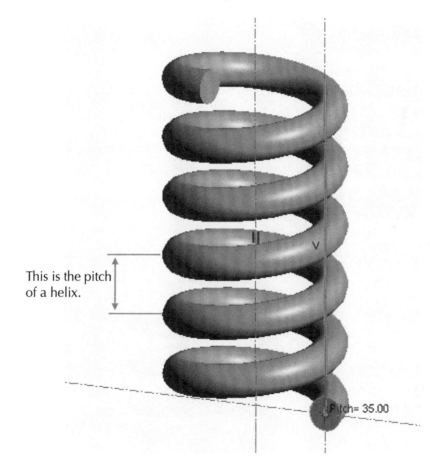

Step 4

A helix can be either clockwise or anticlockwise. Make sure you choose the type you require.

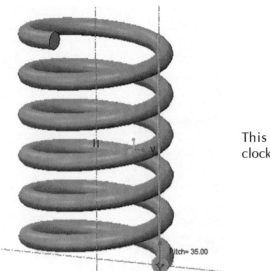

This helix has a clockwise direction.

The same helix has been produced here but with an anticlockwise direction.

Step 5

Finally, either set the length of the helix or define the number of turns the helix has.

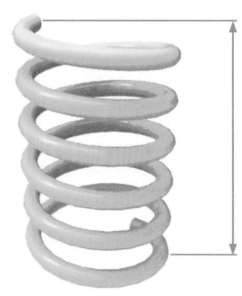

The length of this helix has been set to 200 mm.

With the combination of the length and the pitch used in this example, you can see how the helix starts and ends on different planes. You may have to take this into consideration when creating a helix.

This version of a helix has seven turns. Notice how the helix starts and ends on exactly the same plane.

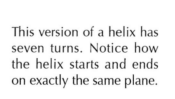

This is one turn. You can see how there are seven turns for this helix.

Intersecting features

It is possible to create a solid from the overlapping parts of two solids.

Here, two square blocks have been extruded. The area of intersection is the square formed at the point where the two blocks cross. This has been highlighted to make it clearer.

This solid is then produced.

Another example is when two elliptical solids are intersected.

This solid is created from the intersection.

An alternative use of intersecting features is shown here.

The 3D CAD model begins with a solid piece of material of the required size and thickness (a blank).

The required profile is then sketched onto this.

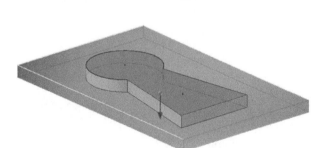

If the intersect command is used now, a solid the thickness of the original blank is produced.

This is particularly useful if you need to produce a model with size restrictions based on material available.

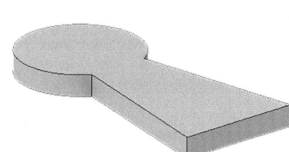

Applying a shell

The shell tool is used to hollow a solid object and create a constant wall thickness. The user must specify the wall thickness they require.

You can select one or more faces of the solid to open up and project the shell through.

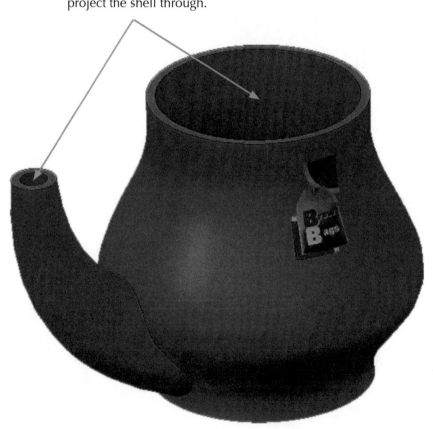

GO! Exam Tip

When describing a shell:

Step 1: State that you will use the **shell** command.

Step 2: Specify the **wall thickness**.

Step 3: If you are opening an end of the solid, identify which faces this applies to.

Applying a fillet to an edge

A fillet will round off an edge on a solid.

A fillet can be applied to both an external and an internal edge.

You can set the radius of the fillet to whatever size you need. This radius can be constant or elliptical.

The edges of the teapot handle have been rounded off using a fillet.

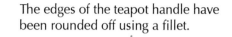 Exam Tip

When describing a fillet:

Step 1: State that you will use the **fillet** command.

Step 2: Specify the **radius**.

Step 3: Select the edges you will fillet.

Applying a chamfer to an edge

A chamfer will add an angle to an edge on a solid.

A chamfer can be applied to both an external and an internal edge.

You can set the size of the chamfer to whatever you need.

You can see that a chamfer has been applied to the outside edge of the wooden box shown here.

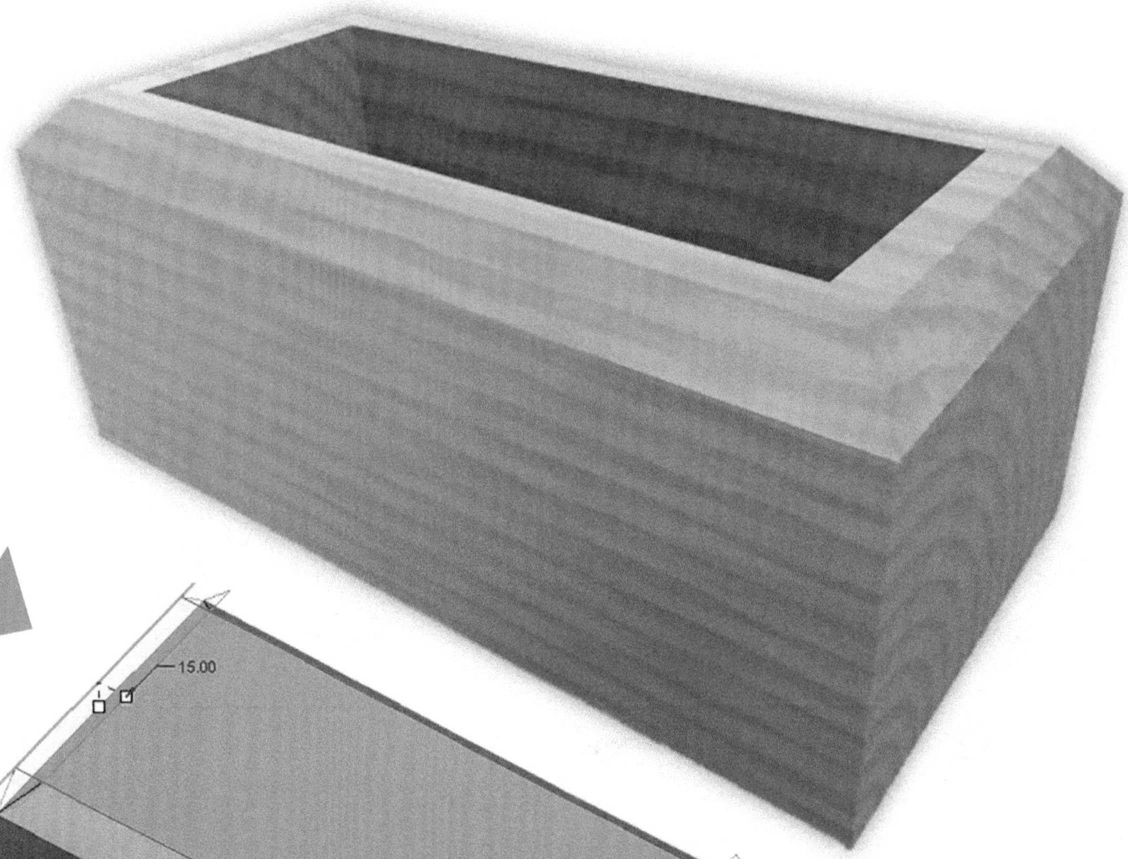

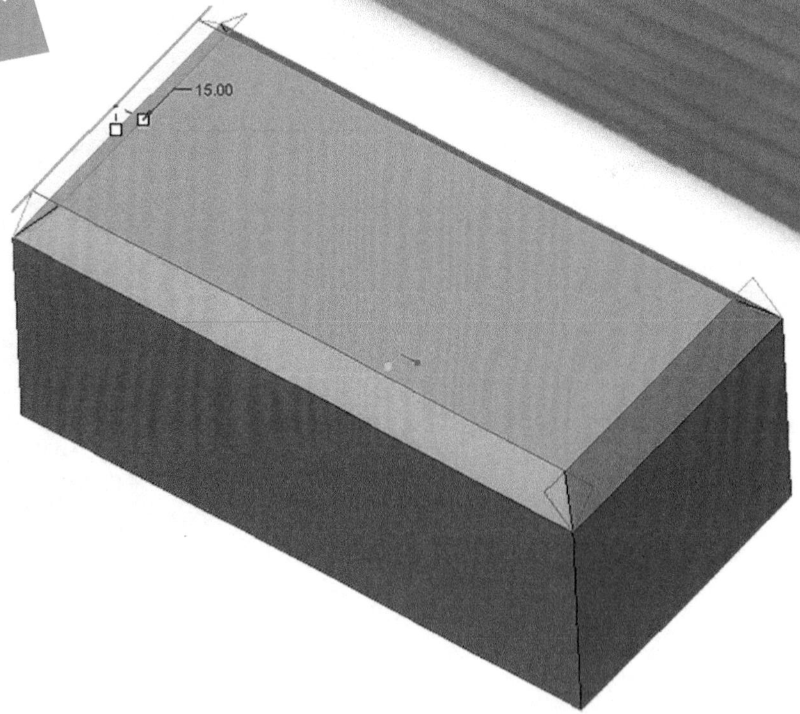

The chamfer tool is selected and the size of the chamfer is set by the user. The edges are selected and then the chamfer is created.

— 15.00

GO! Exam Tip

When describing a chamfer:

Step 1: State that you will use the **chamfer** command.

Step 2: Specify the **size** and **angle**.

Step 3: Select the edges you will chamfer.

The mirror edit

The mirror edit allows a component to be created with a mirror image applied to a defined workplane or face. In the example shown here, a company that manufactures brass nameplates starts with a half shape and then mirrors it to create a symmetrical shape. This allows the company to adjust the overall length of the shape for names of different length whilst maintaining symmetry.

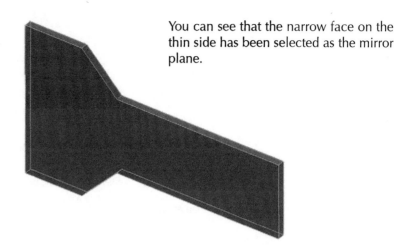

You can see that the narrow face on the thin side has been selected as the mirror plane.

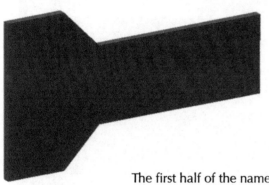

The first half of the nameplate is shown here.

The original half of the 3D model is repeated on the other side of the selected mirror plane.

🔵 Exam Tip

When describing a mirror:

Step 1: State that you will use the **mirror** command.

Step 2: Identify where the mirror will take place. If you need to create a new workplane for the position of the mirror, ensure you include dimensions.

3D CAD MODELLING

Using the array tool

The array tool is used to repeat a feature in a pattern. These patterns can be arranged in different ways. Most commonly they are arranged along a straight line, in a box or in a circular pattern.

Radial array

To create a radial array of a 3D modelled feature, you need to set an axis in the centre of the circle. The feature will already have been created. In this example, the hole is to be repeated in a circle around the base of the teapot.

There are commonly two settings used to specify how the array should be completed: the number of times the feature is to be repeated and the required angle between each feature. Often, the position of the repeated features will be represented by a dot before the settings are accepted. This allows the user to check their work before completing the array.

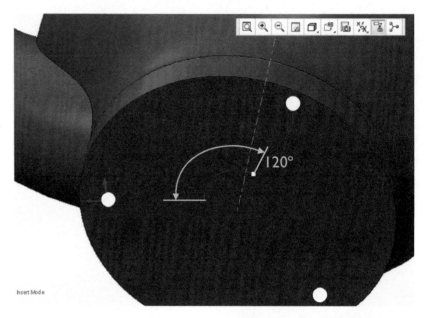

Insert Mode

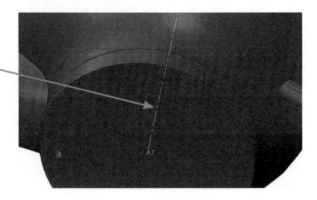

The axis is placed in the centre of the radial array.

The feature can be applied once the required settings are entered.

3D CAD MODELLING

116

Linear array

A linear array allows a feature to be repeated along a straight line with a set distance between the repetitions.

In the pencil holder shown here, the holes for the pencils need to be repeated to make five holes along the top of the aluminium bar.

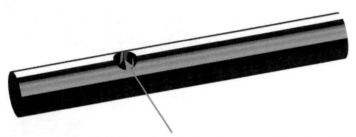

First, the feature needs to be selected, which in this example is the hole. Then the direction of the array needs to be defined.

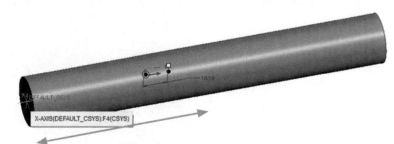

The direction is shown by the coordinate system display.

The number of features and the distance between each of the repeated features needs to be set.

This example has five features with a distance of 20 mm between each of them.

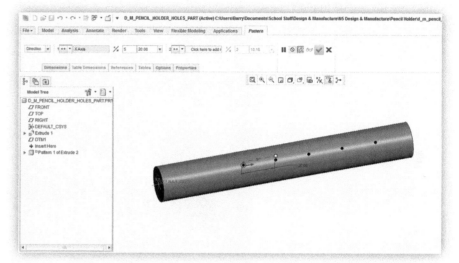

3D CAD MODELLING

Box array

A box array allows a feature to be repeated along the x-axis and the y-axis in the pattern of a box.

This key holder shows the results of a box array.

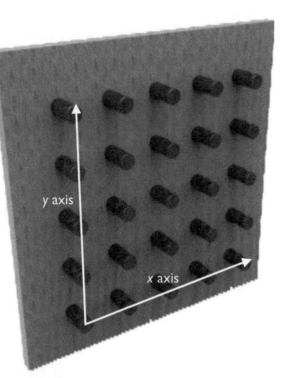

y axis

x axis

Step 1

The original feature is one peg created at the bottom corner of the board.

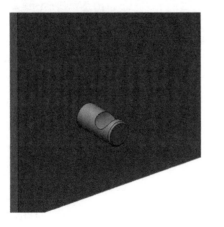

Step 2

Once the feature has been selected, the array can be set. The two directions are set by selecting edges of the solid. Then the settings for the distance between each repetition and the number of repetitions are entered.

Often, the software will show a preview of where each feature will be repeated using dots.

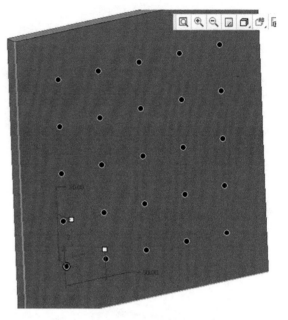

Step 3

In this example, the box array is completed once the pegs are created in the pattern required.

GO! Exam Tip

Step 1: State that you are using a **box array**.

Step 2: Define the features and/or edits you are going to repeat.

Step 3: Define the **directions** of the array.

Step 4: Set the **dimensions** of the spaces between the repeated feature in **each direction**.

Curve array

A curve array will repeat a 3D form along a curved path.

The first step is to create the solid form. In this case, a cylinder has been created for fence posts.

🔵GO! Exam Tip

You will not be asked about this type of array in your exam. It is included in this book to help you create more advanced models.

Next, a curve for the path of the array has to be sketched.

The parameters for the curve array are entered into the option boxes.

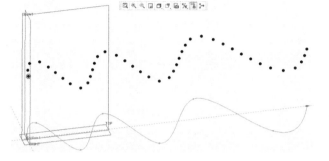

The array will be previewed on the screen. The positions of the solids will likely be represented by black spots.

The completed curve array is shown here.

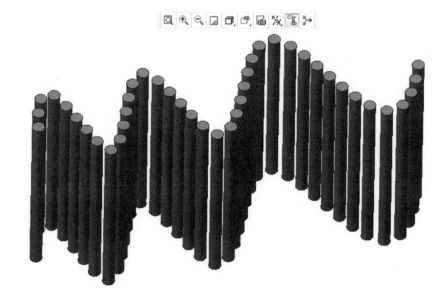

Constraints are helpful drawing tools that can assist the production of CAD models by giving some feedback on the types of line or shape being sketched. These constraint symbols will automatically appear while drawing shapes. This will help you to create 2D CAD shapes within the sketching area of 3D CAD modelling.

Linear

A linear constraint will lock a straight line to a vertical or horizontal direction. Usually a small H or V is used to signify the lines as being horizontal or vertical.

V

H

It can also be used to help the user draw lines along the same horizontal or vertical plane.

This is often shown by small lines on the sketch.

Perpendicular

A perpendicular constraint will lock a line at right-angles to another line. This is often indicated by a symbol on the sketch.

Radius or diameter

This constraint allows the radii or diameters of circles in a sketch to be locked at a specific size. This is useful where a number of circles of the same size are required, as only one needs to be dimensioned.

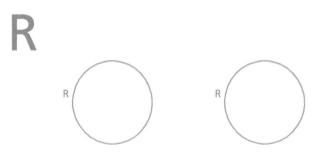

R

R   R

Parallel

A parallel constraint will lock lines in parallel to one another. This is useful, especially when drawing angled lines.

This constraint is shown by two small angled lines beside each of the straight lines being drawn.

Tangent

A tangent constraint will snap a circle or straight line to the tangent point of another circle.

This is often shown by a T.

Concentric

A concentric constraint will help to draw circles with the same centre. The cursor will snap to the centre of a previously drawn circle to ensure accuracy.

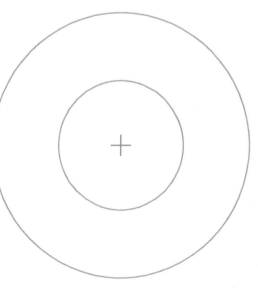

🔵 GO! Assignment Advice

Using these constraints will help you produce accurate 3D CAD models when working on your assignment. Develop your knowledge of them during your coursework.

Assembling parts of a model

When creating 3D models of objects, we create the different components as separate files and then assemble them to build up complete products.

This has many advantages:

- It allows more realistic models to be created.
- It allows moving parts to be animated.
- It allows exploded views of the object to be easily created.

The pen shown here has been assembled from its component parts.

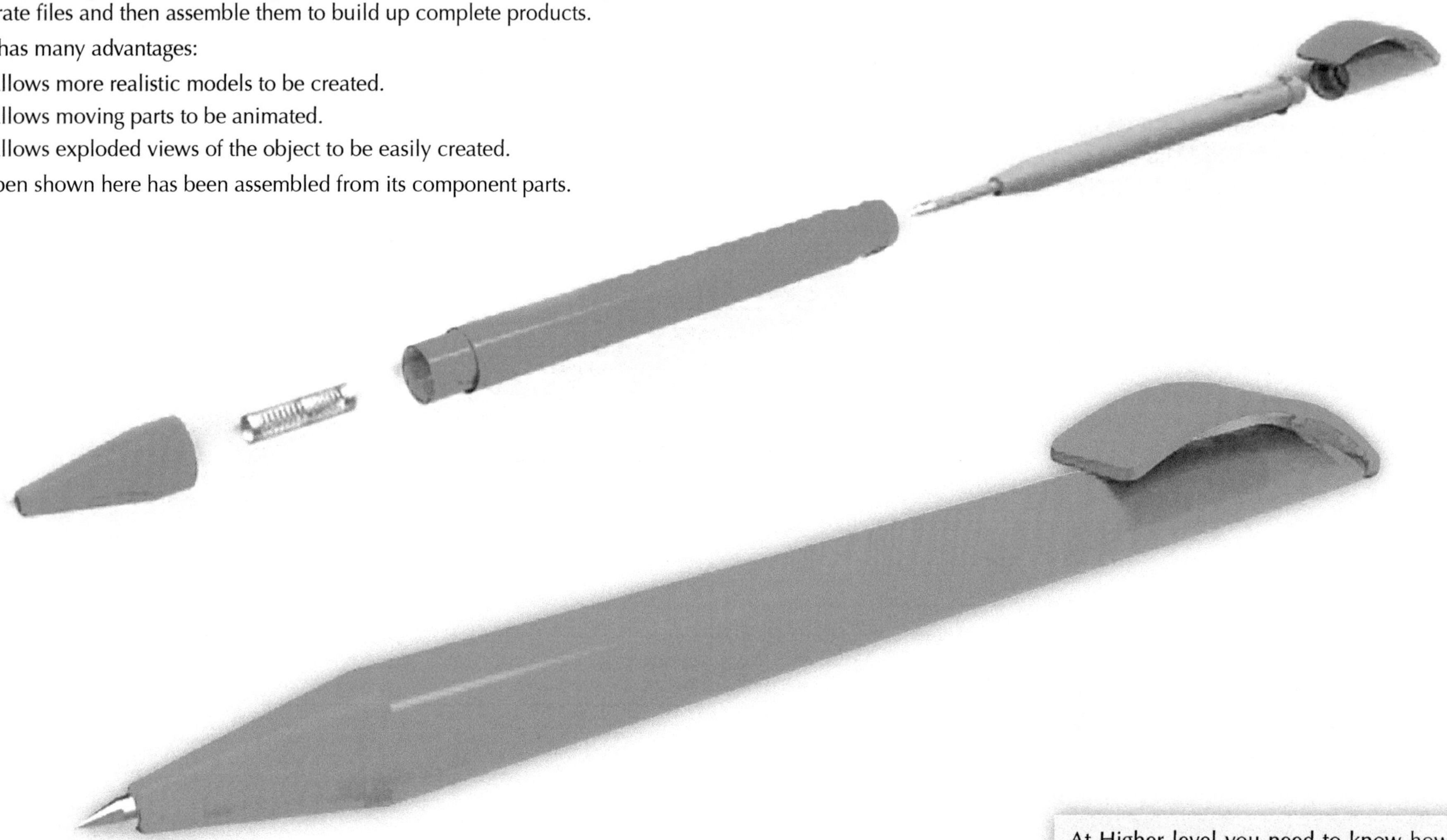

The methods of assembling the different parts are called constraints. These constraints define the relationship between the parts.

At Higher level you need to know how to use the following assembly constraints:

- centre axis
- mate
- align
- offset
- tangent.

Centre axis

When aligning circular objects, the centre axis tool can be used. This will make all the round surfaces line up. It is very useful when you are looking to insert a round bar into a round hole.

Mate

The mate tool makes faces touch each other.

Here, the ink stopper for the pen is to be lined up with the inkwell. The two flat surfaces that are to touch each other are assembled. They are selected and then mated to achieve this.

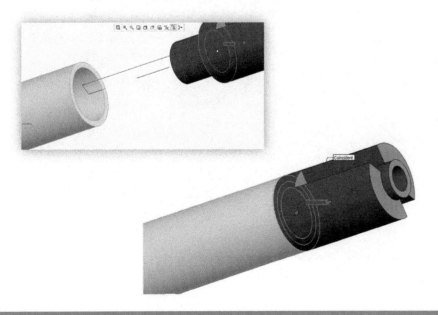

Align

The align tool places faces on the same plane.

You can see the difference between the mate and align command here. The same two faces that were selected to mate the objects (on the left of the page) are selected here.

The align has set the faces on the same plane, rather than lined up to meet each other.

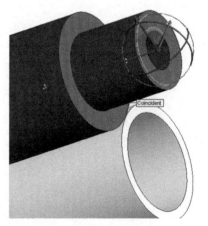

Offset

The offset tool allows the user to set faces at required distances from each other.

Here, the desk has been set to be a specific distance from the edge of the room. The side of the desk and the side of the room are selected in the same way they would be for either a mate or align assembly, but the distance at which they are to be placed is entered.

The two faces here have been selected and an offset has been applied between them.

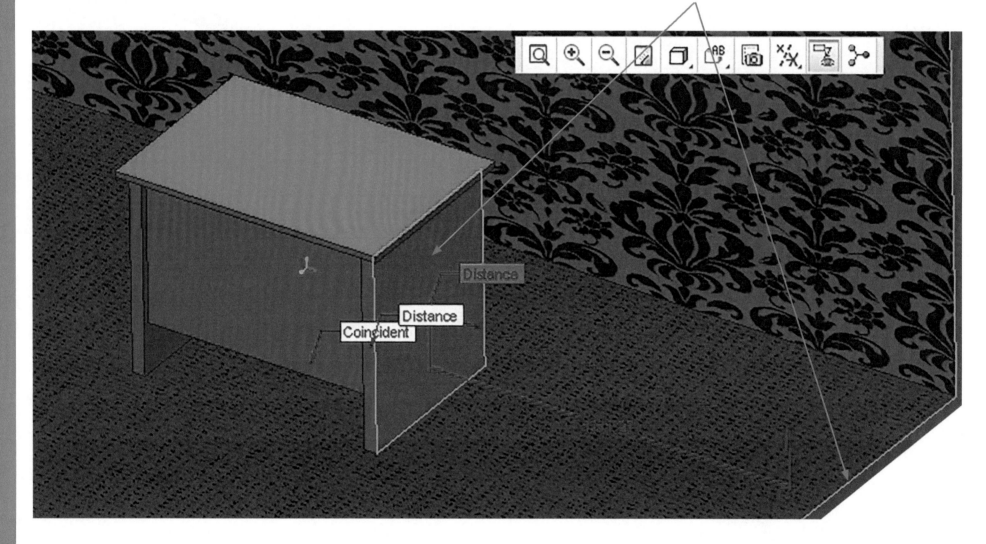

Tangency

The tangency tool allows the user to set curved faces to touch each other at one point only. You can see in the example of the pencil holder here how the curved faces of the tubes are touching.

It is one of the least used assembly commands but can become useful when it is vital to have curved faces touching.

Assembly files

An assembly is a file or 3D CAD model in which two or more parts have been put together to create a complete model of an object.

The footstool shown here was assembled from component parts, which were 3D modelled individually.

There are many advantages of creating 3D CAD assembly files from the individual parts. The moving parts of a model can be simulated within the 3D CAD assembly model and can be animated to show how they work. The materials used for each of the parts can be tested for strength to ascertain whether they are strong enough for the job.

Exploded views are easy to produce from a 3D CAD assembly model. They show engineers how the items in the drawing can be fitted together for manufacture. They are often used in flat pack assembly instructions to help people build their furniture.

Sub-assembly

A sub-assembly is an assembly file that is placed into another assembly file.

In the example shown here, each of the items in the room has been modelled and assembled before being assembled together in the room.

Creating a suitable environment to show items in context is an important part of Higher Graphic Communication. You must develop your skills during your coursework so that you can create high-quality environments when it comes to the assignment.

GO! Assignment Advice

It is likely that you will need to produce an environment during your assignment. You will be provided with STEP/IGES files to use for the environment assembly. You must also be able to apply a decal to surfaces. Make sure you are comfortable with completing these tasks before beginning the assignment.

Stock or library components – CAD libraries

Libraries of premade 3D CAD models are available. These can be accessed through websites or as part of the software program you use.

These CAD libraries save time and effort as the user does not have to create all the components they require from scratch. They also ensure that where standard components are used, they will all be identical.

The scene below uses library components to help show the teapot in context on a stall at a trade fair. Using these components allows the user to make use of other people's expertise and ensures a high-quality production.

🔵 Assignment Advice

The environment you build as part of your assignment should only contain models that were provided by the SQA or that you created yourself during the assignment task.

3D CAD views

Solid model

A solid model view provides a realistic view of a 3D CAD model. Any decals or colour that have been added will be visible on the model. Decals are images that can be added to a 3D CAD model. They will take the form of the model and can be positioned and sized to the user's needs. Materials, reflections and shadows are less obvious and of a poorer quality than on the fully rendered final version of the product.

Wireframe

Wireframe views can be useful to see the structure of a 3D model. It can be more difficult to understand the shape of an object in a wireframe compared to a solid model, but it will show internal detail better. They can help the CAD user to build complex models and ensure parts fit together properly.

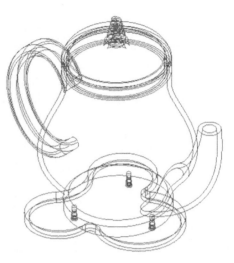

Rendered model

Professional rendering of a 3D model is completed using a specialist rendering package. This provides a photorealistic view of the 3D model that can be used in advertising. Often, the product will be placed in a suitable environment to enhance the look of it. Shadows, reflections and textures are all shown to create a highly realistic graphic.

3D CAD rendering techniques

You will use a number of different rendering techniques when producing promotional graphics. You will set different light sources, add materials to the CAD models, show reflections and shadows and place the model in a suitable environment.

The example below shows an environment for the advertisement of a teapot. The list on the left-hand side shows the different light sources used. The user has specified that shadows will be cast by the light sources. They can also set how bright and what colour each light should be. Any reflective surfaces will show light bouncing from them in a realistic way.

The environment below is shown with wallpaper, carpet and a glass window and offers realistic representations of the materials within the scene.

The materials used in a scene will affect how strong the reflections are and the strength of each of the lights will determine how the shadows appear.

While 3D modelling packages will allow the user to render projects, the quality tends to be fairly poor.

Highly realistic and effective scenes can be created with specialist rendering software.

GO! Assignment Advice

For the best quality, use specialist rendering software to produce your environment.

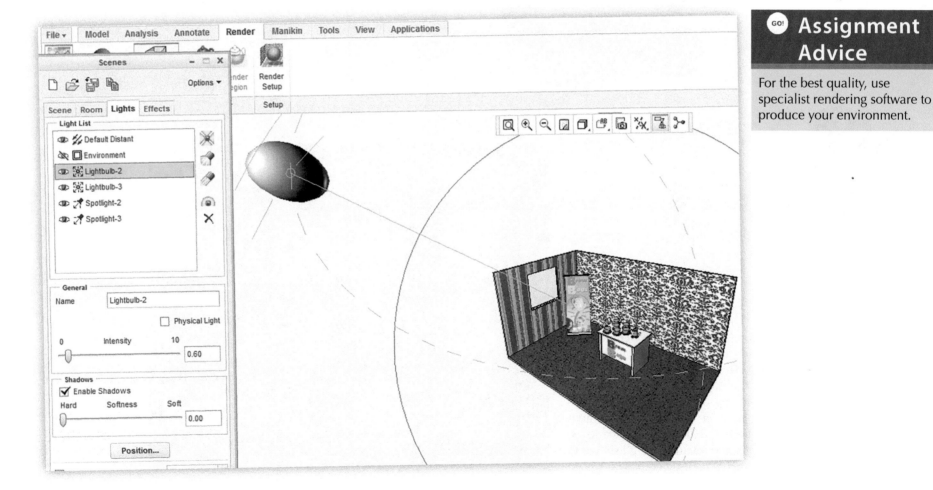

Terms involved in 3D modelling

To use 3D modelling software effectively, and to describe the process accurately, you must be able to use the correct terms.

Faces

Faces are the flat or curved surfaces of a 3D model.

Edges

An edge is the line where two faces meet at an angle.

Vertices

A vertex is a point (corner) on a 3D modelled object where two or more edges meet.

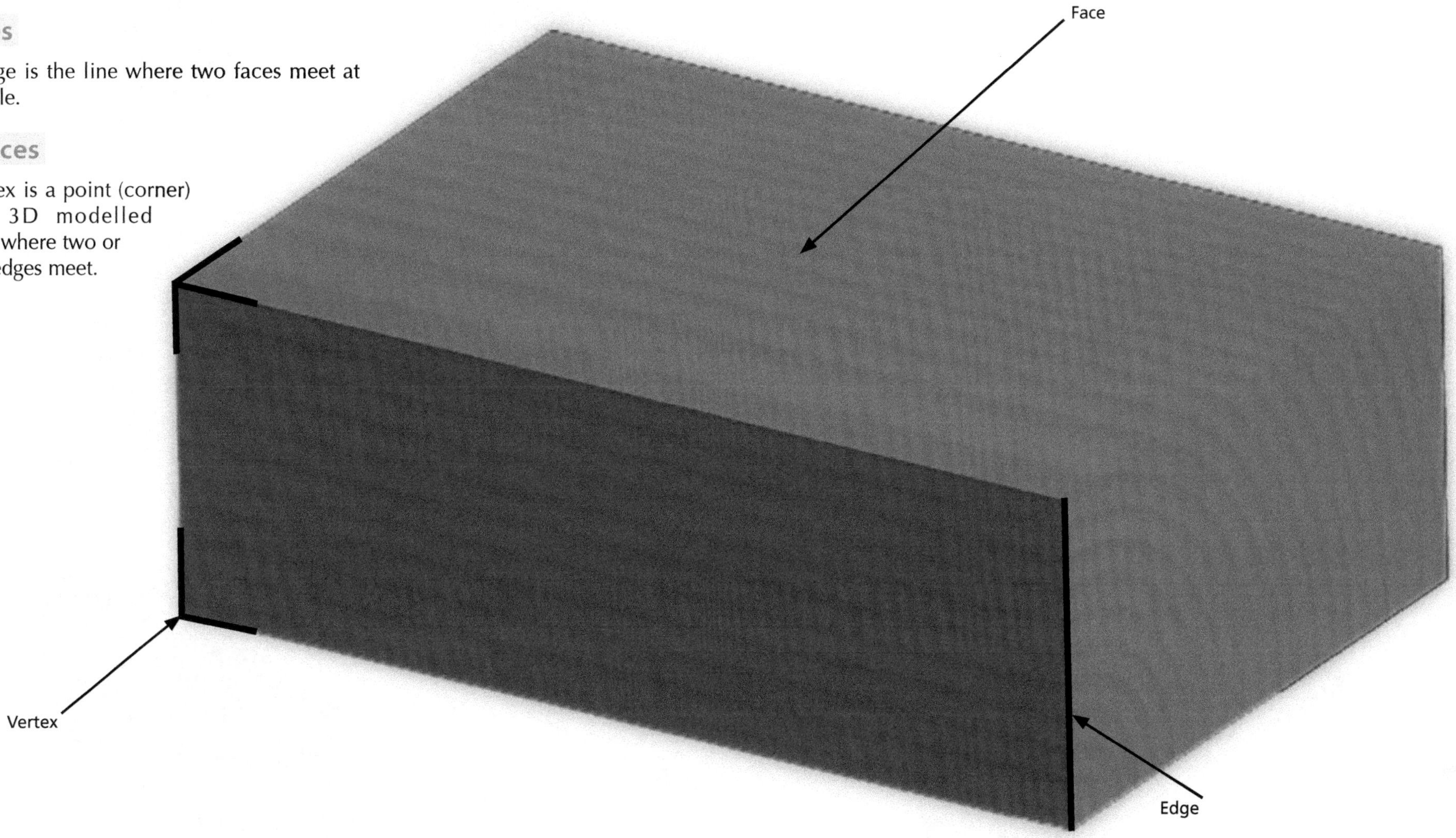

Face

Vertex

Edge

Modelling concepts

Bottom-up modelling

When an object is created by 3D modelling the component pieces separately and then assembling them, it is known as bottom-up modelling.

In this example, the different parts of a child's peg toy have been produced separately as individual parts.

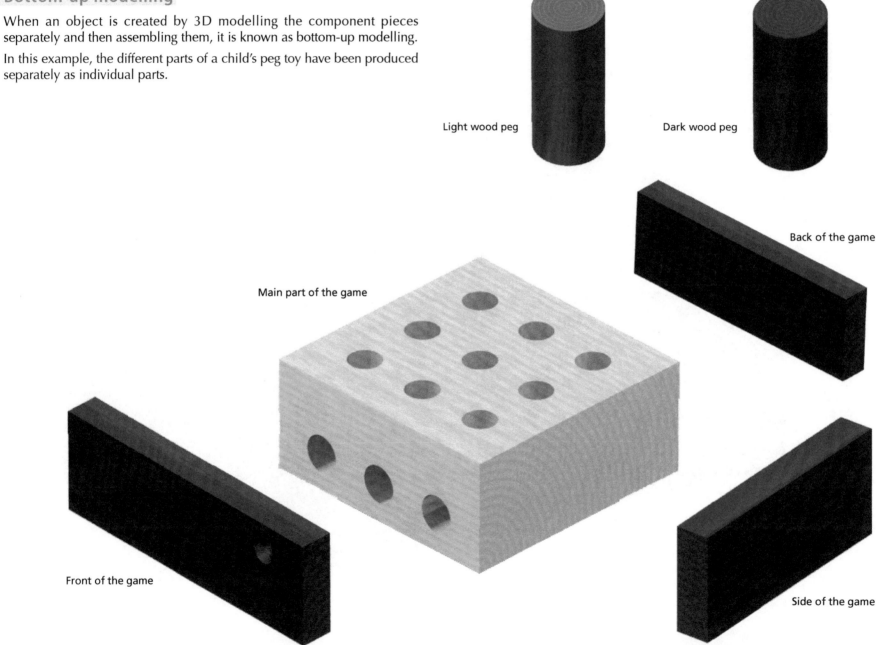

Light wood peg

Dark wood peg

Back of the game

Main part of the game

Front of the game

Side of the game

The different parts of the toy are then assembled using the centre align, mate and align tools.

This method is called 'bottom-up' because you build all of the parts required first and then move on to creating the assembly.

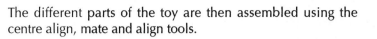

Top-down modelling

When the different parts of a 3D model are built within an assembly around an existing part, it is described as top-down modelling.

This is useful when working with library parts. Some parts of the model can be created in context in order to ensure they accurately fit in place. For example, when a designer is developing new flat pack furniture, the knock-down fittings that will be used to assemble the pieces are supplied in standard sizes. This means that some parts of the furniture can be modelled around the fittings to ensure they fit.

While in an assembly, the user can create a new part. This will be saved as a part drawing, which can be edited individually at a later time if required.

When using top-down modelling, a part is created in context. The other views are ghosted (greyed out) so that the user can see the new part clearly and still use the edges of the other parts of the models. The project tool is extremely useful when creating the part in context, as you can use the lengths from the other parts to ensure accuracy.

A glass, which is to be filled with water, is shown here.

To render this realistically, the water needs to be modelled as a separate part. To ensure that the water fits exactly in the glass, the water has to be created in context using top-down modelling.

First, the glass has to be opened in an assembly file and the option to create a part in the assembly is selected by the user.

The elevation of the glass is shown here.

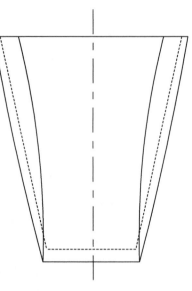

When sketching in context, the outline of the shape is greyed out while the new sketch is drawn. A solid can then be created from the sketch. In this case, the sketch will be revolved to create the water.

Shown is the profile and centre axis for the water to be placed in the glass. The profile will revolve through 360° to create the solid for the water.

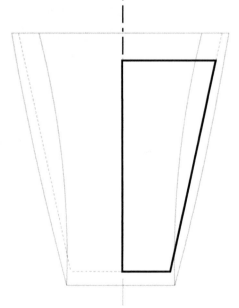

When creating a model in context, the other models are greyed out while the new model is created. This makes it clearer to see the part you are working on while top-down modelling.

Once the part is created, it will be displayed in context in the assembly. In this example, the water has been shown in the assembly with the glass.

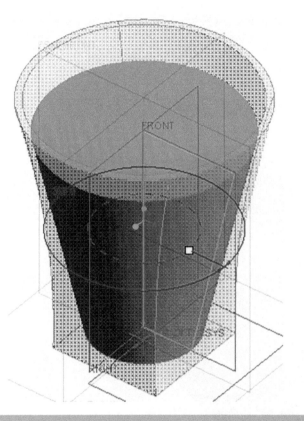

GO! Exam Tip

Top-down modelling means that you can ensure new parts will fit exactly into an assembly. Parts of sketches that have been created based on existing dimensions using the project tool will automatically have their sizes updated if other parts are modified.

3D CAD MODELLING

Modelling tree/hierarchy

A modelling tree or hierarchy shows the different stages followed when a 3D CAD model is produced. This is shown at the side of the model.

It is a very useful tool as it allows you to edit specific parts of your model without having to start the entire thing again. This speeds up the process of developing graphics and provides the opportunity to make real-time changes to the product.

It also allows you to move some of the features so that they occur earlier or later in the model. This can be particularly useful when dealing with the shell command.

GO! Exam Tip

It is common for an exam question that refers to a modelling tree to ask how you would edit an existing CAD model. This is the largest advantage of using a modelling tree, so look out for such questions.

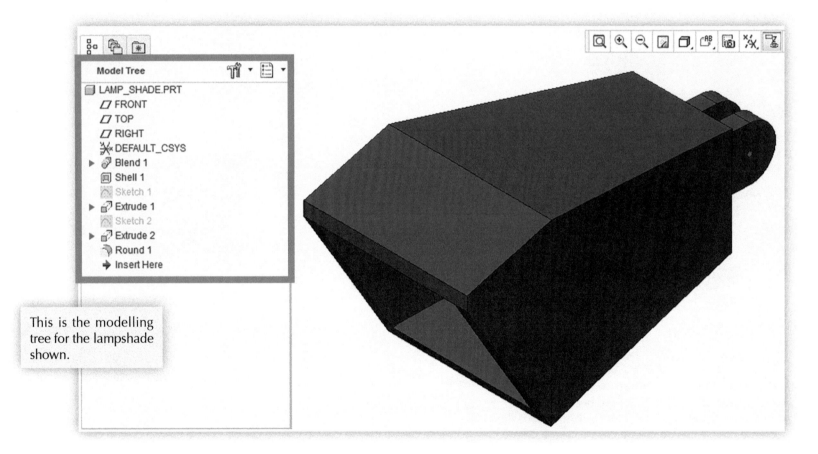

This is the modelling tree for the lampshade shown.

Modelling plan

A modelling plan helps the user to create the 3D CAD model. It should show the sizes used for sketches and features and the order in which the model is created.

You can produce a modelling plan prior to creating a 3D CAD model and use this as evidence. Alternatively, you can produce a modelling plan to describe the stages you went through when creating the 3D CAD model, using screen shots to help illustrate the process.

A modelling plan for how to create a lampshade is shown here.

Step 1

The main solid of the lampshade is created using lofting.

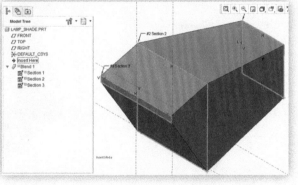

Step 2

The solid is shelled to a thickness of 15 mm. The front face is selected to open it up.

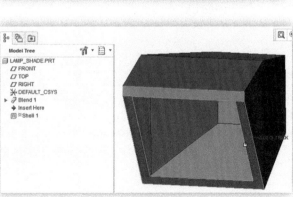

Step 3

The back of the lampshade is sketched, then extruded to length.

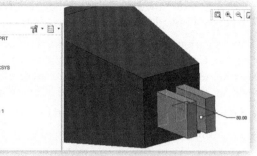

Step 4

A circle is sketched onto the side of this solid, then extruded through both solids to subtract material.

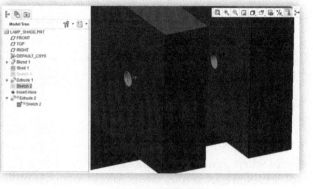

Step 5

The corners of the two solids have a fillet applied to 30 mm.

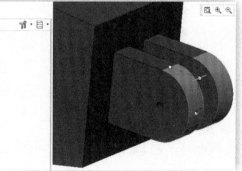

CAD file types

There is a wide range of file types that are useful when producing graphics. They are all linked to various types of drawing packages and purposes.

A wide variety of 3D CAD programs can be used while studying Higher Graphic Communication. Each of these have their own file extensions for the different drawings, models and renderings that can be produced. For the purpose of the exam, you only need to know about the two below:

- **dxf** – This is the file extension used by AutoCAD® for drawings.
- **3ds** – This is a 3DS Max® file for renders.

GO! Exam Tip

Regardless of the software you may use at your centre, you only need to know that a dxf file is a drawing file and that a 3ds file is a file type for a rendered image.

STEP/IGES

STEP and IGES files can be used by any 3D CAD package. This makes them useful when sharing files between different users. During your coursework, you may have used STEP files. For example, if you have produced a stand for a pair of headphones, the stock pair of headphones from the SQA is supplied as a STEP file.

IGES files are an older type of generic 3D CAD file format. They do not have the same information stored in them, such as the volume of an object, and have stopped being developed. STEP files have largely replaced this type of file format.

GO! Exam Tip

You must know that STEP and IGES files are universal 3D CAD file types.

stl

An stl file is a stereolithography file. It converts the mathematical file of the 3D CAD model into triangles. In turn, this allows the CAD model to be physically produced using rapid prototyping or CAD/CAM techniques.

Below is a rendered image of a perfume bottle with the stl file on the right.

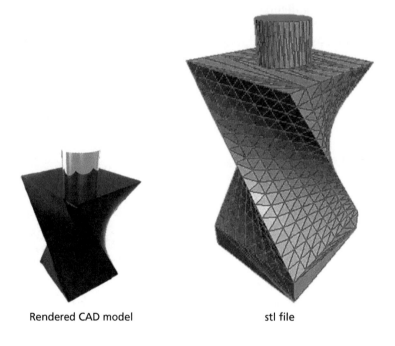

Rendered CAD model   stl file

GO! Exam Tip

Physical models produced from CAD models are a type of technical graphic. They can be used to show a real, physical representation of a product for the client to evaluate before full production begins. Larger 3D printers can be used to produce items ready to be sent to market with only small amounts of finishing required.

CAD libraries

A CAD library is a collection of commonly used shapes and symbols.

They help the user in a number of different ways. They save time and effort, as the user does not have to redraw each shape or symbol every time it is required. They also ensure that the British Standard symbols are used. Where stock parts are required in the design of a product, they ensure that those parts are used consistently.

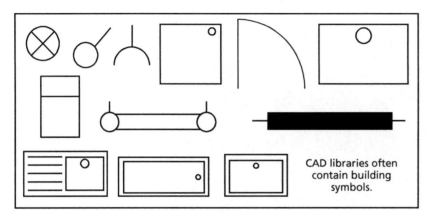

CAD libraries often contain building symbols.

Online CAD libraries will give a selection of components depending on your search criteria.

Online CAD libraries

There are online resources where users can search for stock components. These CAD libraries are stored online and allow members of the online community to upload any CAD model they have created so that it can be reused by other users.

When using these libraries, you can refine your searches by file type. As STEP/ IGES files can be used with any 3D CAD program, searching for these types of files when looking for existing models will ensure that you can use them in your work.

You can use models from online CAD libraries to help build environments for your CAD work throughout the course. If you do use these library models in your work, it is good practice to reference where you got them from. During the assignment, you can only use files provided by the SQA. You must not use an online CAD library at this stage.

GO! Exam Tip

CAD libraries are a collection of commonly used symbols or 3D CAD models. They save the user time by allowing them to select components they require without having to produce them all individually.

BIG **SMOKE**
HELICOPTER

Chapter 7

Desktop Publishing

You will learn

- Desktop publishing
- Planning the layout of promotional graphics
- Planning strategies
- Visuals and annotation
- Proofs (pre-press)
- Magazine page features

Desktop publishing

Desktop publishing (DTP) software is computer software widely used to produce promotional graphics.

The biggest difference between books and magazines is that magazines have to make the information contained within their pages attractive to look at to incite or provoke interest. Magazines are as much about entertaining their audience as they are about informing them.

Magazines are not the only type of publication that make use of DTP. Any type of advertising or communication with customers can be improved with the effective use of DTP. Business cards, bookmarks, roller banners or the interfaces used on touch screen devices are all examples of publications that utilise the design elements, design principles and features of desktop publishing.

Almost every home computer has a DTP package installed on it, which allows a huge number of people to be able to produce some kind of DTP document. There are also websites available that allow people to produce promotional graphics without any knowledge of how to structure an effective promotional document because they provide a variety of templates to use.

There are a large number of terms associated with DTP. Some word processing packages share common features with DTP packages. This means most people will be familiar with some of these terms. However, there can be no doubt that it is better to use a proper DTP package when producing visual layouts.

GO! Assignment Advice

Practise and experiment with how you can use the different DTP features and commands in your presentations to make them look professional.

Text box

A text box is an area into which you can add text. The text will follow the shape of the box if you choose to resize it.

The text box can take the form of any shape you like.

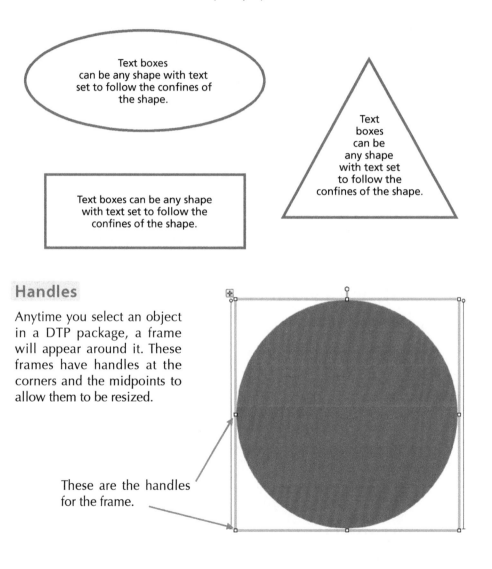

Text boxes can be any shape with text set to follow the confines of the shape.

Text boxes can be any shape with text set to follow the confines of the shape.

Text boxes can be any shape with text set to follow the confines of the shape.

Handles

Anytime you select an object in a DTP package, a frame will appear around it. These frames have handles at the corners and the midpoints to allow them to be resized.

These are the handles for the frame.

Colour fill

Colour fill allows a shape to be filled with a colour specified by the user. There are a number of fill options for colour, e.g. a solid colour, gradient or texture.

Solid

Gradient

Texture

Colour picking

The colour picking tool allows a colour from an image to be sampled and used in any other feature on the DTP presentation. On this business card for a local golf club, the colour of the flag has been picked and used for the colour of the text. This helps to ensure an accent colour is used throughout the presentation to improve its unity.

The colour picker icon is often shown as a dropper in DTP packages.

Textured fill

There are a range of textures that can be applied to a shape when using DTP software. These can be used to improve a presentation in compliance with the design element, texture.

Gradient fill

A gradient fill shows one colour gradually fading to another. The user can adjust the settings to control the colours, pattern and direction of the gradient fill.

This is an effective method of adding tone to a presentation to give it form.

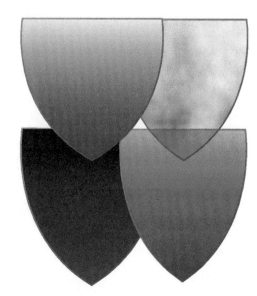

Text wrap

When text follows the edge of an image, it is described as being 'wrapped'. This is a useful method of incorporating images into your presentations and creating unity. Text wrap can also help save space in a busy layout.

There are different types of text wrap available to use in DTP software and you should try to use the most appropriate one. You can see that the text here has been set to wrap around the right-hand side of the image.

Here the text has been set to wrap around the left-hand side of the image.

It is also possible to edit the position of the wrap points around an image. You can see the points are displayed around the image shown here. These can be moved to suit your requirements.

Reverse

Where there is a strong contrast between the colour of the background and the text, it is called 'reverse text'.

These are all examples of reverse text.

Reverse text   **Reverse text**

Reverse text

Extended text

This is the term given to long sections of body text.

The shaded areas here would be the extended text of a magazine article.

Flow text along a path

Text can be set to follow a line or shape.

Text can flow along any path that the user creates.

The flow text function can be used to make the text follow the shape of an image in a presentation, which can help achieve movement and rhythm.

Copy and paste

Copy and paste can be used to repeat an image or frame somewhere else within the document.

Cut and paste

Cut and paste can be used to remove an image or frame from one document or part of the page to another.

Orientation

Orientation refers to the direction of the page, which is usually selected at the beginning of creating a new document. There are two possible orientations:

Landscape

Portrait

Line spacing or leading

The space between lines of text can be enlarged to make it easier to read. This only works to a point, after which the text becomes disconnected and more difficult to read. Conversely, line spacing can also be made smaller to help fit more information into an area of a presentation.

This text has double line spacing.

You can see that the distance

between the lines is larger, which

can make it easier to read or put

handwritten notes into.

This text has condensed line spacing. You can see that this makes it more difficult to read, but that more text can be fitted into a smaller space. This is often used for the small print on contracts.

Transparency

The transparency setting allows objects in a DTP document to be made see-through.

The amount of transparency can be changed to suit the needs of the user.

In the example here, a transparency has been added behind the company logo to make it easier to read on the backdrop of the image.

Cropping (square and full cropping)

The crop tool can be used to remove the outer portions of an image, making it smaller in size. Square cropping is the most simple form. It is often applied to screen grabs, so that only the relevant part is shown.

Full cropping is where only the required part of an image is left. The rest of the image is removed. Usually, this requires work in photo editing software to be successful.

The two images below compare the two types of cropping. The image of the MP3 player on the left has been square cropped. The one on the right has been fully cropped to the outline of the MP3 player.

This is the original poster.

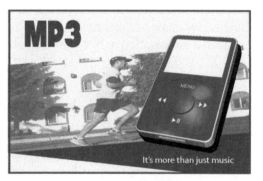

Square cropping   Full cropping

Drop shadow

When a shadow is applied behind text or an image, it is called a drop shadow. This will add depth by making it look like the object is coming off the page.

DTP software allows the user to edit the various aspects of the shadow such as its intensity, direction, colour and sharpness.

It is a simple yet effective way of adding depth to a page.

DROP SHADOW

GO! Assignment Advice

Study the layouts of a wide range of magazines in order to help you develop your own ideas. You can either buy these or use free magazine or newsstand apps.

Rotate

The rotate setting allows you to turn an image through an angle. The user can select from preset angles or has the option to input any angle they require.

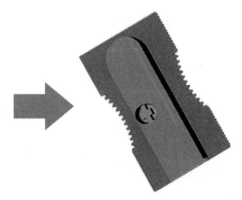

Paper sizing

The physical size of a page can be altered. A smaller page size can be used to reduce printing and transport costs. This can also make a magazine or newspaper easier to read and carry. Some layouts need to be larger in size, like roller banners or large posters.

The most common set of paper sizes in use are the ISO A sizes. These range from A0 (the largest) to A8. The size is reduced by half each time.

In school, A4 and A3 are the most frequently used paper sizes.

A4 paper is 297 × 210 mm.

A3 paper is 420 × 297 mm.

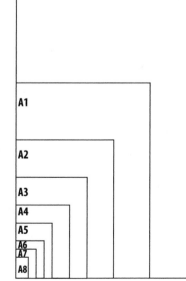

Alignment

There are five main types of alignment:

1. Top alignment

2. Bottom alignment

3. Left alignment

4. Right alignment

5. Centre alignment (horizontal or/and vertical).

Alignment is often used to add structure to a DTP layout so that it is easier to follow and looks visually organised. Effective use of alignment will help the reader to follow a DTP layout as it was intended to be read.

Alignment can create a visual connection between various elements of the layout, which makes it clear that these elements, e.g. text and an image, are linked. Where sections of text belong together, or where text belongs with an image, alignment can be used to help show this relationship.

Alignment can also be used to help create and maintain rhythm in a presentation. Where sections of text belong together, or where text belongs with an image, alignment can be used to help show this relationship.

Look at how alignment is used in the magazine layout opposite. Two examples are labelled.

All of this gives the layout structure and makes it easy to read and understand.

GO! **Exam Tip**

If you are asked about alignment in your exam, make sure you refer to a specific type of alignment in your answer. Simply saying object A is aligned with object B is not enough to gain you marks.

The headline and the body text are left aligned.

The blue box and the grey box are right aligned.

Single- and multi-page formats

Multi-page layouts include magazines, folding leaflets and tabletop advertising. They all consist of more than one page.

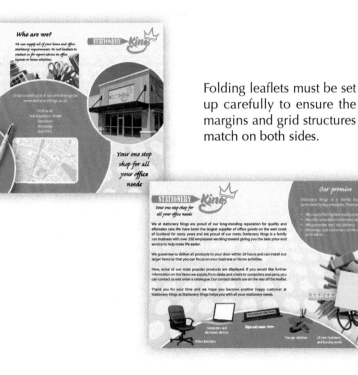

Folding leaflets must be set up carefully to ensure the margins and grid structures match on both sides.

Examples of single-page layouts are posters and business cards. These layouts are often best kept simple to have strong visual impact.

Justification

Even though they are similar, there is a difference between alignment and justification that you should be aware of. Alignment is how different parts of a layout line up with one another. Justification refers only to text and how it is set out.

Text can be justified in four ways:

1. Left justification   **3.** Centre justification

2. Right justification   **4.** Full justification

Left-justified text begins each line at the left margin.

Right-justified text begins each line at the right margin.

Centre-justified text is measured from the centre of the column or page.

Fully-justified text is aligned to both the left- and right-hand margins as shown here. This can make the text look ordered and tidy. However, the gaps between the words and characters will be different on each line. This can make fully-justified text more difficult to read than text that is justified to only one side.

Grid

A grid is a pattern that the user can set on the DTP layout page, which helps to structure the layout.

Grids can be regular or irregular in pattern. The choice will be determined by the type of publication being produced. Formal layouts usually follow a strong grid structure, whereas informal layouts can use irregular layouts to have greater visual impact.

Snap

When you set up a grid or ruler guides, you can make the cursor snap to these marks as you create your DTP presentation. This speeds up the process of laying out your DTP work and can help to ensure alignment with images and text.

This shows a master page layer with a grid and guides. The cursor will snap to each of the red lines to help achieve accuracy and consistency of layout throughout a book.

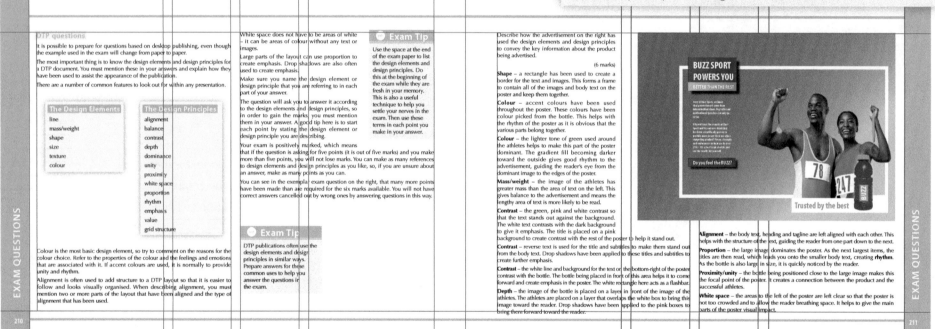

Guides

A guide is a line that is shown on the screen to help position text or graphics. These lines are not printed in the final version of the document.

Master page layers

Layers are parts of a DTP document, which contain the different elements of the presentation. You can view the individual layers, a selection of layers or all the layers together.

Master pages allow you to structure all of the pages in a magazine or book on the same grid format. These allow consistency of layout to be achieved easily.

Serif and sans serif

There are two families of font available for you to use: serif fonts and sans serif fonts.

Serif fonts tend to be more traditional and formal, while sans serif fonts are more modern and informal.

Serif fonts have small serifs (small lines) on the ends of each letter. Sans serif fonts do not have these serifs. The term 'sans serifs' means 'without serifs'.

Serif

These are serifs

Sans Serif

Font styles

Font styles can be used to infer the use and target market of the product being advertised or a feeling or emotion.

Horror

Childlike

Love

ELECTRONIC

Medieval

Futuristic

Indent

An indent is where a selected part of body text starts further in from the left margin than the rest of the text.

> This piece of text has been indented by 20 mm from the left margin.

Indents can be used to highlight parts of text that may be of particular interest to the reader or to show the start of a new paragraph.

Hanging indent

A hanging indent is where the first line of text is not indented, but the rest of the lines are. These are commonly found where there are lists. A useful application of this is in a DTP presentation when describing the product specification of an item.

> Often pupils back up their school work using a USB memory stick. This is because:
>
>   it is portable
>   it has large storage capabilities
>   it is cheap.

Drop caps

Using the drop caps feature highlights the first capital letter of a passage and makes it bigger. This makes the first letter stand out, giving it impact and helping to lead the article on from the larger subheading text.

In this week's edition of Beatz, we look at the rise of Scottish DJ 'DeeJay Choon' and how one track has elevated him from unknown to an international superstar.

Running headline

A running headline is a header that appears on each page of a DTP document. It can also be referred to as a running header. Running headlines often contain the title of the book or chapter or the name of the magazine.

Study guide	DTP terms

Import/export

When creating DTP documents, it is possible to import or export different types of files.

You can import pdf files into some DTP software packages for editing and can also import images.

It is also possible to export files from a DTP document. For example, you can publish an entire DTP document as a pdf file so that it can be viewed using any computer. This function can also be used to export a DTP document as an image file.

DTP layers

The different parts of a layout are called layers and can be ordered to create the best possible effect. Parts of a layer can be partially hidden behind other layers or brought to the front.

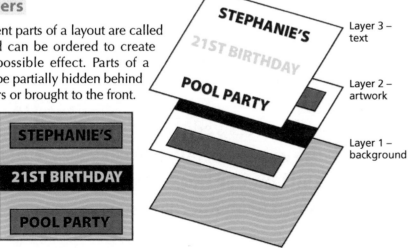

STEPHANIE'S
21ST BIRTHDAY
POOL PARTY

Layer 3 – text

Layer 2 – artwork

Layer 1 – background

Before you can produce your final presentation, you should plan different ideas for how it will look.

This will enable you to explore various possibilities so that you can create the most effective possible layout.

Creating new ideas is difficult. As shown in the diagram below, creating is the most difficult type of thinking we can do. This is why engineers, designers and people working in the creative industries are well paid and well qualified. Using the process described over the next few pages will help you with the creative process of preparing promotional graphics.

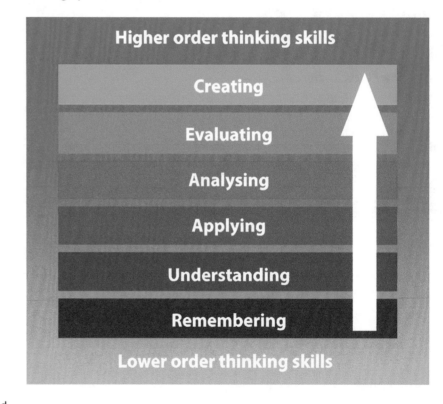

Higher order thinking skills

Creating

Evaluating

Analysing

Applying

Understanding

Remembering

Lower order thinking skills

Planning strategies

When a client approaches a graphic designer to complete some work for them, they will give the designer a brief. This brief will outline the type of graphics required, their purpose and the target audience. Only if the brief is well written by the client will the graphic designer be able to produce a range of suitable images.

A structured method of planning layouts can help you to produce high-quality presentations:

1. Thumbnails

2. Visuals

3. Proofs

Thumbnails

Thumbnails are quickly produced ideas for the layout of a presentation. The examples shown here have been produced using manual methods, but thumbnails can be produced using electronic methods. From the initial ideas produced at this stage, some will be developed into the visuals produced using DTP software.

Using a curved line to separate the company name from the rest of the presentation helps give it dominance.

Using the image of the teapot at an angle helps to break the formality of the structure to give it impact and emphasis.

Bleed used for the teapot will attract attention to the product.

Using the lines through the diagonals will add to the rhythm of the layout and give the company name dominance over the layout.

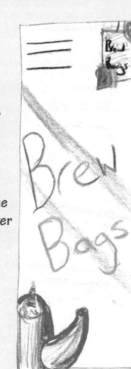

Including the company logo is important to promote the brand.

Using a flashbar behind the teapot will bring it forward to give it prominence.

This is a simple layout structure, which is clear and effective.

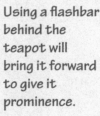

The position of the company logo between the text will add unity between these areas.

The contrasting colours used with the teapot and background make the image more eye catching.

The areas of text are right aligned with each other to give the presentation good rhythm.

The company name is positioned centrally to allow it to dominate the layout and connect all the elements.

Visuals and annotation

Visuals are better quality representations of the final idea for the presentation. They are produced using DTP software to give a quality output at speed. The images used at this stage may be of a lower quality than in the final presentation.

GO! **Assignment Advice**

Using digital methods to plan your DTP layouts will help you gain marks in your assignment. This is because it will be quicker for you to develop these thumbnails into the final layout, giving you more time to develop the layout into a high-quality piece of DTP work.

Annotating the visuals as they are produced can help you to improve the structure and organisation of the thoughts and processes that naturally take place. This makes it easier for you to make the appropriate improvements and optimise the evolutionary process.

Version 1

Company colour scheme has been applied throughout the presentation.

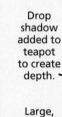

Brew Bags images used to promote the product identity.

Text and company name is left aligned to create a more organised look and to make the sub-heading easier to read, following on from the heading.

Asymmetrical alignment is used to create movement and interest.

Teapot contrasting with the company colours to create impact.

Teapot placed in front of arcs to create depth.

Version 2

Brew Bags name prominent at the top of the poster. There may not be enough contrast between the name and the background for it to stand out.

Drop shadow added to teapot to create depth.

Large, dominant image of the product to create impact and be eye catching.

Large positive image of the target market to create dominance and positive feeling toward the product.

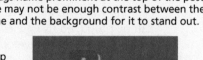

Left-aligned text to help rhythm.

Brew Bags logo bleeds onto page to create impact.

Version 3

Centre alignment has been used with the Brew Bags name, the teapot, the slogan and the image at the bottom of the presentation to create rhythm. This leads the viewer from the top to the bottom of the banner quickly.

A drop shadow has been added to the teapot and the text to make them stand out. The use of dark and light drop shadows helps to differentiate the teapot from the slogan. The light drop shadow makes the slogan easier to read and makes it lighter in weight to give it the feeling that it is floating off the page.

The text has been turned at an angle to give a feeling of excitement to the presentation. This is eye catching and also leads the reader from word to word, providing the presentation with rhythm.

The large brand name dominates the presentation which draws attention to it.

A transparency has been added to the background to help the Brew Bags name contrast with it so that it can stand out.

The slogan above the teapot helps to present the teapot in a frame and separate it from the dominant company name at the top of the presentation.

Image of teapot overlaps the layer of the circles. This makes it stand out and creates unity between the top and bottom sections of the presentation.

Transparent white box displayed behind the logo to help it stand out against the image.

Positive image of target market bleeds into the bottom of the presentation to create impact and good balance.

Product identity reinforced with the brand logo placed in the corner.

Proofs (pre-press)

Proofs are the final version of the presentation, which have to be checked by the customer and editors before going to print. Any mistakes must be picked up at this stage. The people who do this job must be very thorough in their checks and have a good eye for detail.

The proof is evaluated against the original brief and specification. Only if it meets the specification will it be deemed appropriate for a print run.

Brief

You need to develop preliminary, production and promotional graphics for a proposal for a teapot.

You must provide:

- preliminary sketches that convey material, light and shade for the teapot designs
- dimensioned orthographic drawings for the teapot
- technical detail required to manufacture the teapot
- pictorial line drawings of the teapot to help show non-technical people how it appears to fit together
- promotional material to advertise the teapot. This should be a 150 × 600 mm roller banner that can be easily transported to be used at trade fairs and shopping centres.

You must also display the teapot in a suitable environment to show it in context.

This layout meets the brief:

The image of the young women makes it obvious that the company is aiming the product at young people.

The Brew Bags logo and colours are used throughout the layout to emphasise the company identity or brand.

The use of text at angles creates impact and reflects the fresh look that this range of teapots is bringing to a traditional product.

The Brew Bags company font, Jagger SF, is used throughout the presentation.

The presentation shown is a scaled representation of the real-life roller banner.

Magazine page features

Magazines have their own particular set of features that can be used to make them attractive and have visual impact.

Headline

A headline is the main heading of the presentation. It is normally the largest text size on the sheet and dominates the other pieces of text.

Margin

The margins are the spaces between the columns and the left- and right-hand edges of the page.

Subheading

A subheading is usually included in a magazine layout. It is the part of the page that leads the reader from the title to the body text. It gives a short introduction to the content of the article.

Column

Columns are produced when text is set using ordered grid structures. There are many different ways of laying out the columns in a presentation. You should use the one that most suits the style you are trying to achieve.

Pull quote

A pull quote is a small section of text that is sampled and enlarged. This is then set into the layout as a way of attracting interest in the article. It is often set in italics or reverse to make it stand out. Often, it is a controversial quote or an interesting part of the article to entice the reader.

Bleed

After printing, pages are trimmed to size. A bleed is when an image or element runs outside the margins of the page (beyond the crop marks). This means that when the page is trimmed, the artwork or element goes right to the edge of the page.

Gutter

A gutter is the gap between columns of text. It can be kept at a uniform distance for formal presentations or can be altered for more impact.

Column rule

A column rule is a line that runs between two columns to help separate the text. It is commonly used in formal magazine layouts where the text is small in size and tightly compacted.

Caption

A caption is a description or quote that accompanies an image.

Header and footer

A header is the space at the top of a presentation and a footer is the space at the bottom. On a multi-page layout like a book, it is common for the header and footer to be in the same style on every page.

Folio

The folio is the name given to the page number. This can be added to the presentation wherever you want, but is commonly part of the header or footer.

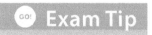

Exam Tip

Ensure you can identify and describe these features, as you can be asked about these in your exam.

Headline

Subheading

Gutter

Pull quote

Floating element

Column

Left margin

Image

Bleed

Right margin

Reverse

Caption

Light

it's in your hands

We take a look at the impact torches have had on our world.

Initially, torches were made from wood, with one end made from flammable material to give light from fire. Over the ages, this has evolved and electricity now powers our torches today.

Possibly the most famous torch in the world, the Olympic Torch, was burned throughout the duration of the games, originally held in Ancient Greece. It commemorates the theft of fire from the Greek god Zeus by Prometheus and was introduced to the Olympics in 1928.

If a torch is made of sulphur mixed with lime, the fire will not diminish after being plunged into water. Such torches were used by the Ancient Romans and would quite possibly have been useful for discovering geological treasures hidden underground.

Torches have also been used in symbolism for generations. It is the symbol of enlightenment and can most famously be found being held by the Statue of Liberty.

Modern electric torches come in many different forms but have improved the supply of light. Head torches used by

miners are a safer alternative to the paraffin lamps previously used.

Interestingly, torches have even given whole communities identities. The people of Newcastle and Sunderland have a famous rivalry, with their nicknames based on the manufacturing of the lamps used by miners. The coal miners in Newcastle were provided with 'Geordie' safety lamps designed by George Stephenson in 1815, while the coal miners in Wearside would make them (make'em) themselves. Hence, Newcastle folk are known as Geordies while residents of Sunderland are referred to as Mackems.

> "The people of Newcastle and Sunderland have a famous rivalry, with their nicknames based on lamp manufacturing"

Large spotlights, like the one pictured, help searches for missing people, while tiny keyring torches, which use high-power LEDs, can help folk find their way home after a night's entertainment.

Modern design has improved how we are able to see in the darkness. Night has almost become day in our ever-frantic world.

Dr I. Ball is an expert on torches and led the design team responsible for the new spotlight from UCTorches.

Large spotlights, like this one by UCTorches, help searches for missing people.

A brief history of light

Light has been a staple part of human life throughout time. So when did the major breakthroughs happen?

70000 BC – Animal fat burned to create light.
3000 BC – Egyptian invent the candle.
1780 – Oil lamp first produced.
1867 – Fluorescent lamp first demonstrated.
1880 – Edison produces 16W lightbulb, lasting 1500 hours.
1962 – LEDs developed.
1991 – Phillips invents efficient lightbulb lasting 60000 hours.
2011 – First LED street lighting installed in the UK in Somerset.

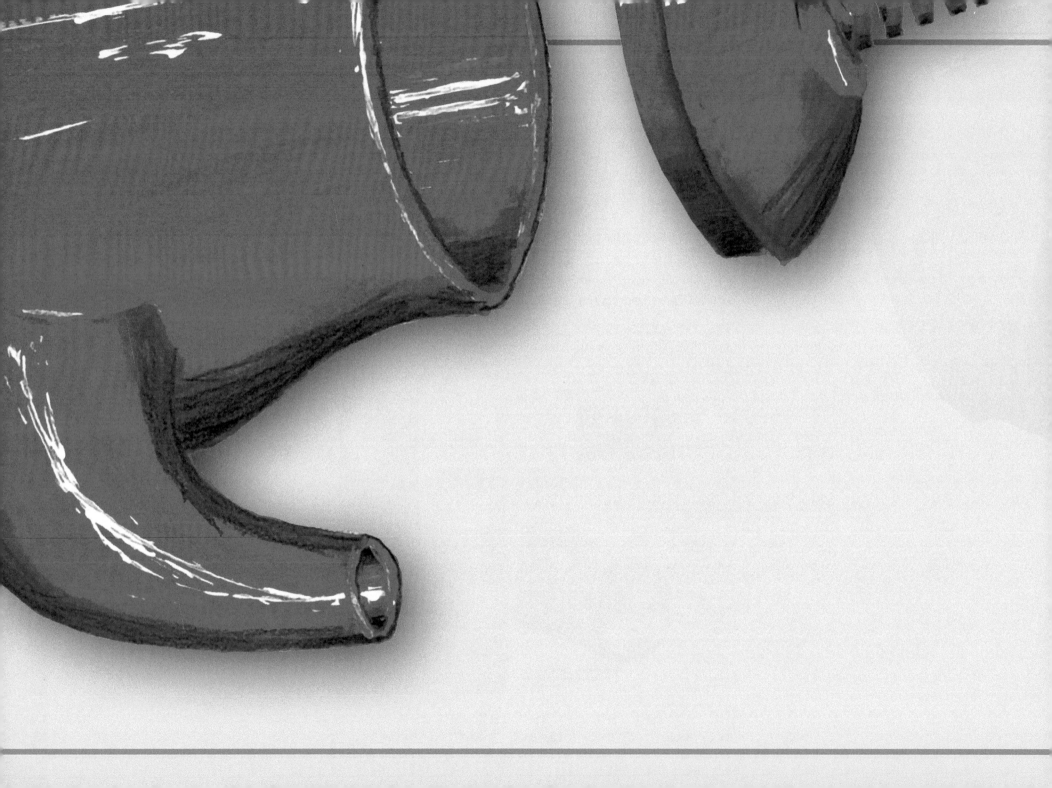

Chapter 8

Coursework

You will learn

- **Meeting the course specification**
- **Scented project**
- **Carabiner clip project**
- **Percolator project**
- **Tazza Lighting project**

Meeting the course specification

The course specification is the document that describes all of the knowledge and skills you need to learn when working through Higher Graphic Communication. The course specification details what will be covered in the exam and the assignment.

Your teacher will organise your course in order to cover the content contained within the course specification in a way that gives you the best possible chance of a good grade.

They will prepare you for the assignment by providing coursework structured in a similar way to how the assignment must be produced. You will have the opportunity to develop the skills needed to produce the types of drawings that will gain you marks in your assignment.

Your teacher will also ensure you are ready for your exam by helping you understand the topics described within the course specification.

It is an excellent study tip to keep a copy of the course specification as you work through the course and mark which areas of study you are good at and which areas you need to develop your knowledge in. This will help you to prepare for the assignment and to revise for the exam.

> The course specification can be found in the Higher Graphic Communication course page on the SQA website: https://www.sqa.org.uk/sqa/47929.html

GO! Exam Tip

Print a hard copy of the table of skills, knowledge and understanding needed for the course assessment from the course specification. Go through the table and indicate the topics you are good at and those where you need to develop your knowledge. Colour code this with red for 'speak to my teacher for further clarification', yellow for 'need to develop' and green for 'comfortable with the topic'.

This section of the book contains some exemplar tasks that you could work through to help you develop your skills and knowledge of the course specification. Worked examples are provided to give you an idea of the type of skills you should be developing as you work through the course. Note that references to STEP files being supplied are to mirror the language you will encounter during your course. If you wish to complete any of the tasks outlined and need STEP files, appropriate images can be obtained from the GrabCAD website (https://grabcad.com). The projects can also be accessed at www.collins.co.uk/pages/Scottish-curriculum-free-resources. These can be downloaded free of charge for you to work through independently or for your teacher to use during your course.

The tasks outlined in this section will prepare you for both the exam and the assignment.

Scented project

This project introduces the various 3D CAD commands that you need to know while working through Higher Graphic Communication. Your teacher will demonstrate how to use the commands, and you will then be able to experiment with these and move on to modelling a perfume or aftershave bottle, to your own design, using all of the commands.

(This unit of work could be used as evidence for exceptional circumstances as it mirrors the assessed work for the course.)

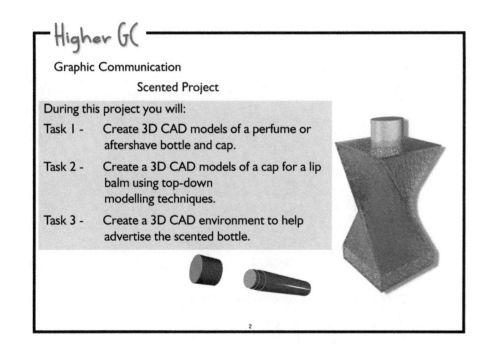

Task 1
3D CAD modelling – Perfume bottle

A perfume company called Scented is releasing a scent for both men and women. The bottle is to be made from glass and the lid from metal. Scented has specified that a design feature of the bottle is that it must have a twist in it.

One possible design is shown to help you. You have also been provided with example production drawings for this bottle.

You should complete the following tasks.

1. Create 3D models of both the bottle and the cap then assemble the two parts.

2. Produce component orthographic views, using third-angle projection, for both the bottle and the cap, which include:
   i) hidden detail
   ii) sectional views of both the bottle and the lid
   iii) an enlarged detail view.

3. Produce orthographic assembly views of the bottle and cap using third-angle projection. These must include a sectional view. Do not show hidden detail.

4. Produce an isometric assembly and an exploded isometric view of the bottle and cap. Do not render these views.

5. Produce a render of the assembly. As an extension task, try to fill the bottle with a clear liquid to simulate perfume/aftershave and render this.

6. Create a rendered environment that shows the bottle in context. You may use CAD models from a CAD library or create your own.

GO! Exam Tip

Regardless of what software you use, describe the 3D CAD modelling techniques using the terms used in this book. This will make exam revision easier as you will already be familiar with the terms that are accepted in the exam.

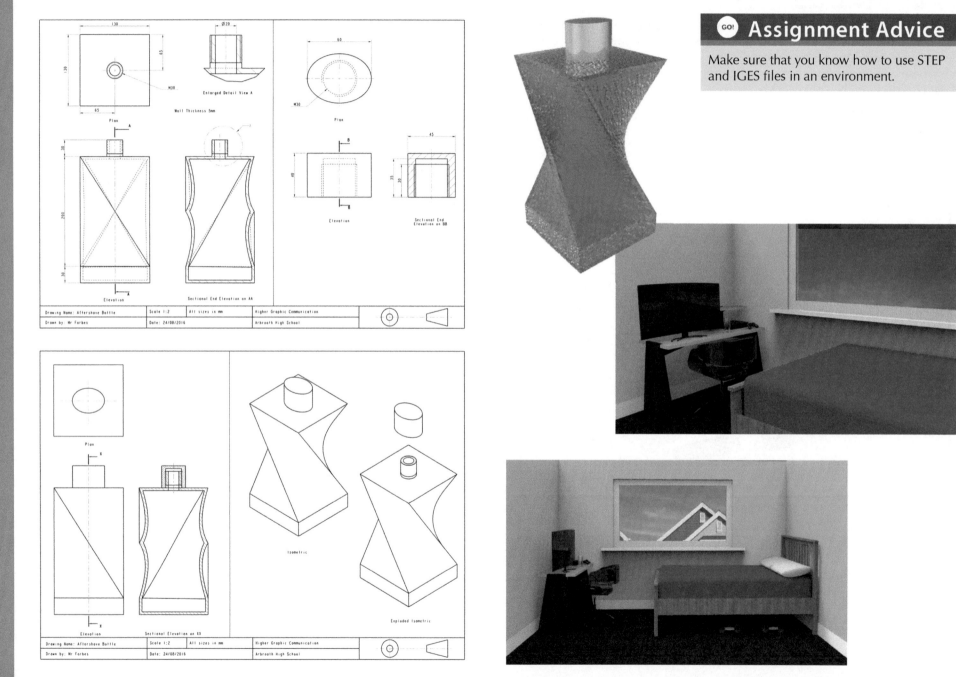

Assignment Advice

Make sure that you know how to use STEP and IGES files in an environment.

Task 2
Top-down modelling – Lip balm

Scented has also produced a lip balm. It has designed the casing but needs to redesign the lid as it was found to be slipping in the user's fingers.

Your task is to design a lid for the lip balm that fits the casing and has a method of gripping it. You should create this lid in context using the top-down method.

The STEP files for this lip balm casing will be provided for you.

The existing lip balm is shown here.

To complete this task you need to:

● create a 3D model of the new cap in context.

COURSEWORK

Carabiner clip project

This project develops skills in manual sketching and rendering. You will also further develop skills in 3D CAD modelling following structured drawings.

(This unit of work could be used as evidence for exceptional circumstances as it mirrors the assessed work for the course.)

Task 1 – Preliminary graphics

Produce sketches of a carabiner clip. Use the carabiner clip your teacher will give you. Use a ruler to find out the dimensions of the clip.

Do not measure your sketches. You may use a straight edge and/or grid paper to help you produce these sketches.

You must produce:

(a) Component orthographic sketches of the various parts of the carabiner clip. Use third-angle projection. Show all hidden detail.

(b) Assembly orthographic sketches. Produce a plan, sectional elevation and an end elevation. Use third-angle projection. Do not show hidden detail.

(c) Two different types of pictorial sketches of the assembled carabiner clip. These must be rendered to show material. One of these sketches must be two-point perspective.

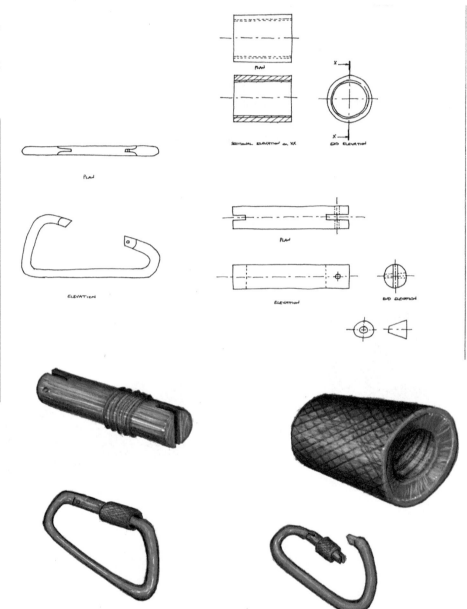

These are worked examples of the type of work you should be able to produce in a task similar to this.

Task 2 – Production graphics

Create 3D CAD models of the carabiner clip. Use the information in the Task 2 data sheet, below.

From these models, produce:

(a) Component orthographic drawings of the parts of the carabiner clip. Show all hidden detail. Show enlarged detail views where required. Show enough dimensions to allow the clip to be manufactured.

(b) Assembly orthographics of the carabiner clip. You must show the plan, sectional elevation and end elevation. Do not show hidden detail.

(c) An assembled isometric and an exploded isometric drawing of the carabiner clip. Do not show hidden detail.

You must use third-angle projection. Produce these drawings as line drawings.

Higher GC

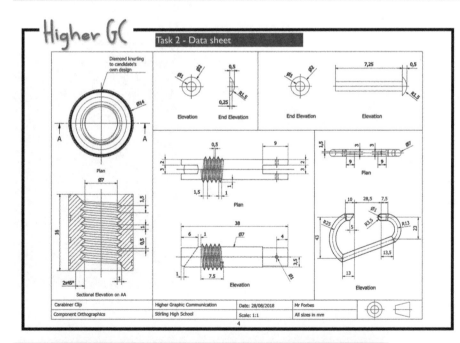

Assignment Advice

Ensure you include all centre lines in your production drawings.

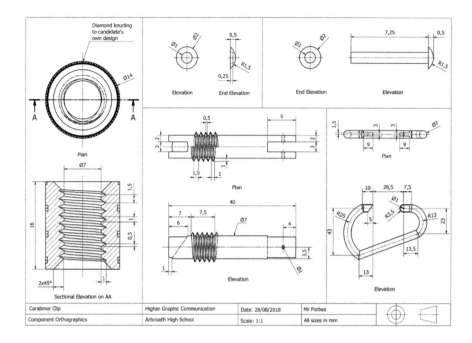

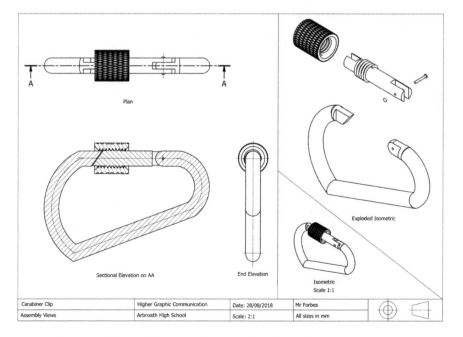

Task 3 – Promotional graphics

The carabiner clip is to be made from metal. At least two different colours must be used to make it more eye catching.

(a) To show how the carabiner clip looks, you must create a CAD render of the carabiner clip.

(b) In order to advertise the carabiner clip, you must create a three-fold tabletop advertisement to promote the clip in a shop. This advert must be completed in landscape format, 330 mm long × 250 mm high.

You must produce two thumbnails to help plan this tabletop tower. You have been provided with a range of images. You are not permitted to use any other text, images or items unless you create them yourself.

You must include a product name, an image and some body text in these thumbnails.

You must identify six design elements and principles that you have used in each of these thumbnails.

(c) You must produce a full-size visual for this. Fully annotate the visual, justifying why you have used your chosen six design elements and principles.

(d) The client would like to see the carabiner clip and the tabletop tower in context.

You will be provided with a STEP file of the tabletop stand to help you place the carabiner clip in an environment. This environment must consist of a shelf in the corner of a room. You should place the STEP file of the tabletop stand onto this shelf. You must incorporate the clip into the environment in any way you choose, e.g. you could hang it on a wall hook or lay it on the shelf.

Render all parts of the environment and show the final layout you produced in **(c)** on the tabletop stand in your rendered environment.

An example of a three-fold tabletop stand is shown

🔘 Assignment Advice

When rendering the 3D CAD model, create a png and set the render options to create a transparent background. This will save you time because you won't have to crop the render.

GO! Assignment Advice

If you are asked to identify design elements/principles in a layout, you should simply state the element or principle and point to where it has been used. If you are asked to justify its use, you should describe how you have used it and the effect it has on the layout.

GO! Assignment Advice

Learn some typical responses about the effect of different design elements/principles before your assignment begins. You can then edit these answers to suit the DTP layout you produce to give you a good chance of earning marks for this part of the assignment.

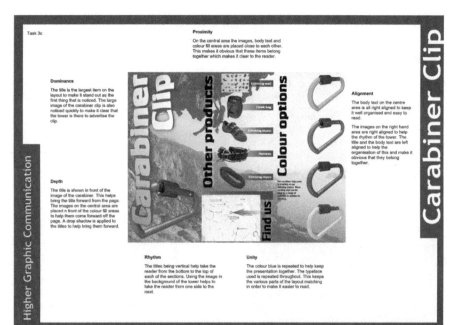

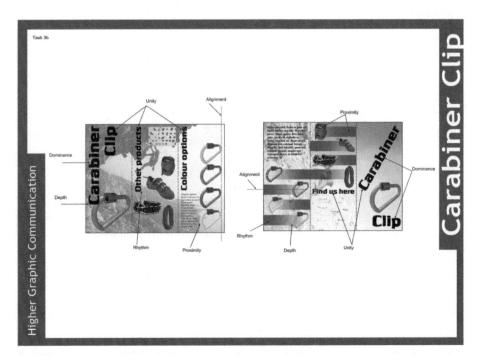

GO! Assignment Advice

Make sure you know how to add decals to multi-faced models. The decals should smoothly fit around the faces on a model such as the table topper shown.

GO! Assignment Advice

Produce an environment exactly as asked for in the assignment. Do not use any models you did not create within the assignment task. If you do, you will receive no marks for your environment.

Percolator project

This project will help you prepare for the assignment and develop your knowledge of preliminary, production and promotional graphics. It will enhance your understanding of the relevance of these types of drawings and how and why they are produced.

You will also cover other areas of the course during this project, such as manual sketching and rendering, dimensioning, tolerances, British Standards, DTP terms and design elements and principles.

You will analyse an existing percolator and create drawings, CAD models and promotional work from this.

(This unit of work could be used as evidence for exceptional circumstances as it mirrors the assessed work for the course.)

Higher GC

Task 1 – Preliminary graphics

Study an existing coffee percolator. Measure the different parts of the percolator and use these measurements to produce sketches of the parts, making sure they contain enough detail to produce 3D CAD models of each part.

(a) Produce orthographic component sketches of the parts of the percolator. You must show all hidden detail in your sketches and use third-angle projection.

(b) Produce rendered pictorial sketches of the percolator. Also, sketch and render any other parts of the percolator you wish to bring attention to; this will help prepare for 3D CAD modelling of it.

Task 2 – Production graphics

Study an existing coffee percolator. Use the sketches you produced in Task 1 to create 3D CAD models of the various parts of it.

From these models, produce:

(a) Component orthographics of the parts of the percolator to a suitable scale.

You must use third-angle projection. Show all hidden detail. Show suitable sectional views of each component. Show enlarged detail views where required. Show enough dimensions to allow each component to be manufactured. Produce these drawings as line drawings.

(b) Assembly orthographics of the percolator to a suitable scale. You must show the plan, sectional elevation and end elevation. You must use third-angle projection. Do not show hidden detail.

(c) An assembled isometric drawing and an exploded isometric drawing of the percolator at a suitable scale. Do not show hidden detail. Produce these as line drawings with no rendering or shading.

3

Higher GC

Task 3 – Promotional graphics

In order to show how the coffee percolator looks, you must:

(a) Create a CAD render of the assembled percolator. Render these parts using the materials in the percolator you have studied.

(b) Create a leaflet for the percolator that will be supplied in the box when it is bought. This leaflet must be completed in landscape format, A4 size. You must complete both sides of the leaflet. Your final visual must be produced to a scale of 1:1. You must use the company colours in your promotional work.

You must produce two thumbnails of both the back and front sides of the leaflet to help you plan this leaflet. You have been provided with extended text and images that you must use. You are not permitted to use any other text, images or items unless you create them yourself.

You must identify six design elements and principles that you have used in each of these thumbnails.

(c) Produce a visual for this to a scale of 1:1. Fully annotate this visual, justifying why you have used your chosen six design elements and principles.

You must include three or more of the supplied images and the supplied body text in your layout.

(d) The client would like to see the coffee percolator in context. You will be provided with a range of STEP files to help you complete this task. You must use only the supplied STEP files and the percolator in your environment, along with the DTP work you produced earlier in the task. You should place the percolator into the environment. All parts of the environment must be CAD rendered to show a realistic scene showing material, lighting, shadows and reflections.

4

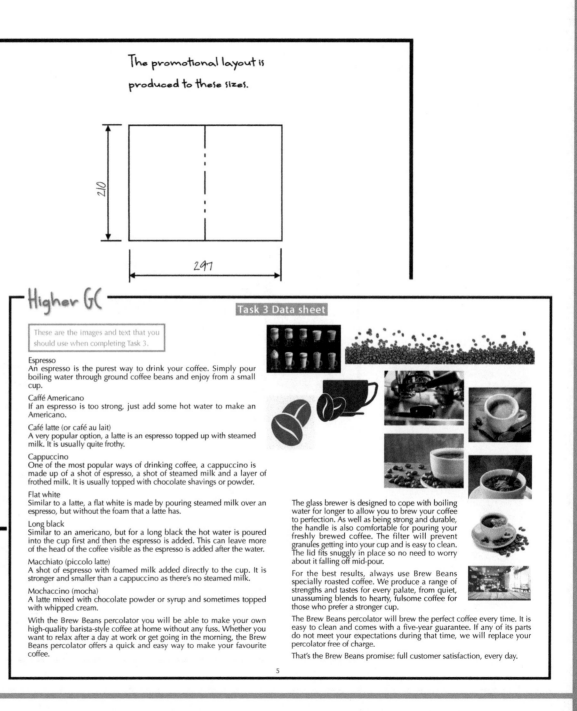

The promotional layout is produced to these sizes.

210

297

Higher GC

Task 3 Data sheet

These are the images and text that you should use when completing Task 3.

Espresso
An espresso is the purest way to drink your coffee. Simply pour boiling water through ground coffee beans and enjoy from a small cup.

Caffé Americano
If an espresso is too strong, just add some hot water to make an Americano.

Café latte (or café au lait)
A very popular option, a latte is an espresso topped up with steamed milk. It is usually quite frothy.

Cappuccino
One of the most popular ways of drinking coffee, a cappuccino is made up of a shot of espresso, a shot of steamed milk and a layer of frothed milk. It is usually topped with chocolate shavings or powder.

Flat white
Similar to a latte, a flat white is made by pouring steamed milk over an espresso, but without the foam that a latte has.

Long black
Similar to an americano, but for a long black the hot water is poured into the cup first and then the espresso is added. This can leave more of the head of the coffee visible as the espresso is added after the water.

Macchiato (piccolo latte)
A shot of espresso with foamed milk added directly to the cup. It is stronger and smaller than a cappuccino as there's no steamed milk.

Mochaccino (mocha)
A latte mixed with chocolate powder or syrup and sometimes topped with whipped cream.

With the Brew Beans percolator you will be able to make your own high-quality barista-style coffee at home without any fuss. Whether you want to relax after a day at work or get going in the morning, the Brew Beans percolator offers a quick and easy way to make your favourite coffee.

The glass brewer is designed to cope with boiling water for longer to allow you to brew your coffee to perfection. As well as being strong and durable, the handle is also comfortable for pouring your freshly brewed coffee. The filter will prevent granules getting into your cup and is easy to clean. The lid fits snuggly in place so no need to worry about it falling off mid-pour.

For the best results, always use Brew Beans specially roasted coffee. We produce a range of strengths and tastes for every palate, from quiet, unassuming blends to hearty, fulsome coffee for those who prefer a stronger cup.

The Brew Beans percolator will brew the perfect coffee every time. It is easy to clean and comes with a five-year guarantee. If any of its parts do not meet your expectations during that time, we will replace your percolator free of charge.

That's the Brew Beans promise: full customer satisfaction, every day.

5

Percolator project – Pictorial sketches

Preliminary sketches are graphics that can show a range of possible solutions to a brief. They can be produced using both manual and electronic methods, as long as 3D CAD software is not used. You must not create preliminary drawings by using software to generate 2D views from a 3D CAD model.

Preliminary drawings give an idea of shape, material, form and texture and are useful to inform the client at the early stages of developing a product.

Throughout the course, you will develop your skills in graphic techniques when producing preliminary drawings.

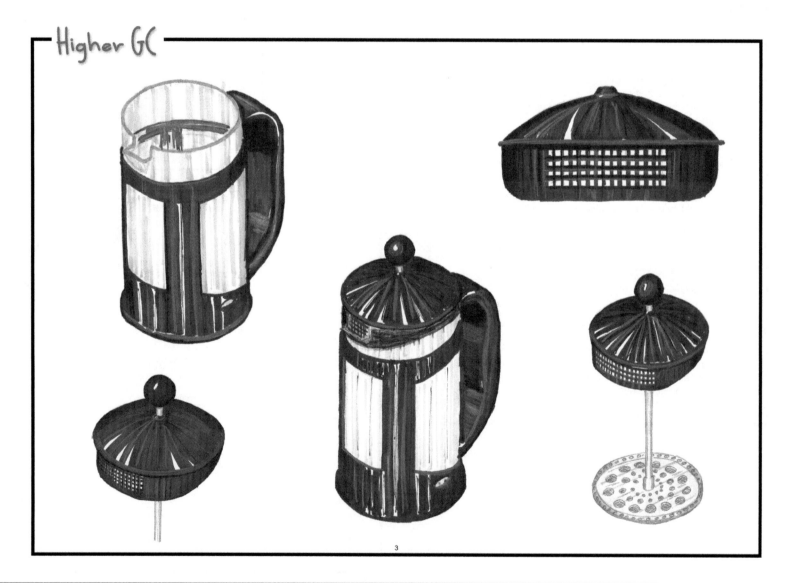

Higher GC

Percolator project – Orthographic sketches

One reason for producing orthographic sketches is to enable you to create the 3D models of the various components of your product. To do this, they will need to contain enough dimensions.

Orthographic sketches also allow a client to view the proposed product from more simple two-dimensional views. This can be important to gain an idea of scale. For this reason, these sketches must be produced to good proportions.

You should practise throughout the year to develop your skills in producing orthographic sketches.

GO! Assignment Advice

Produce your sketches to good proportions in order to accurately convey information about the product graphically to the client.

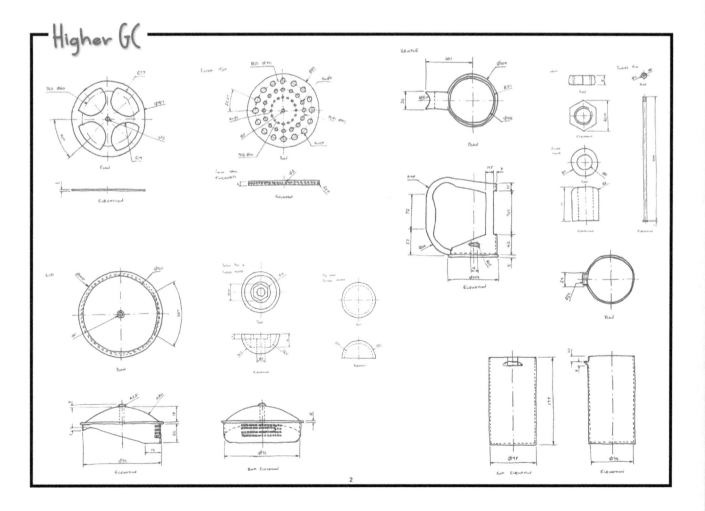

Percolator project – Component orthographics

Once you have 3D modelled the components of the product, you can produce the component orthographic views of each of the parts.

As these are component views, they are dimensioned to allow manufacture. Other details such as centre lines, labels and titles should be included. Use your master sheet to create these drawings.

GO! Assignment Advice

Use your master sheet as a template for all the production drawings you have to produce in your assignment. This will ensure that your sheet is correctly set up to use the third-angle projection method. It will also have a suitable title block that you can complete the details of. This will allow you to focus on completing the assignment task rather than having to spend lots of time changing settings and having to draw a title block, border and third-angle projection symbol during the assignment.

GO! Assignment Advice

Make sure you produce these drawings to the scale specified in the assignment task. Check that you have included all centre lines and dimensions and any required detail views or sectional views.

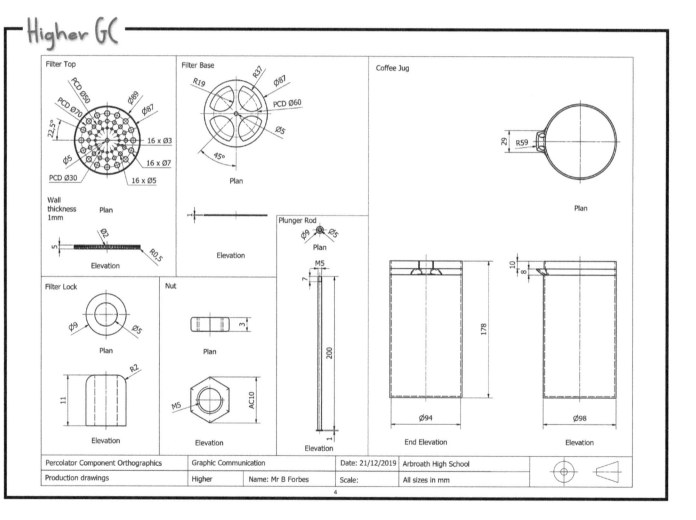

It is likely you will require more than one sheet to produce all of the production drawings required within a project. Ensure that you use suitable scales for all components. Do not try to squeeze too many views onto one sheet, otherwise you will not be able to show enough detail or dimensions for each part.

GO! Assignment Advice

To ensure you include enough dimensions to enable each component to be 3D CAD modelled, you will need to study the data sheets and show all dimensions included on these sheets on your drawings.

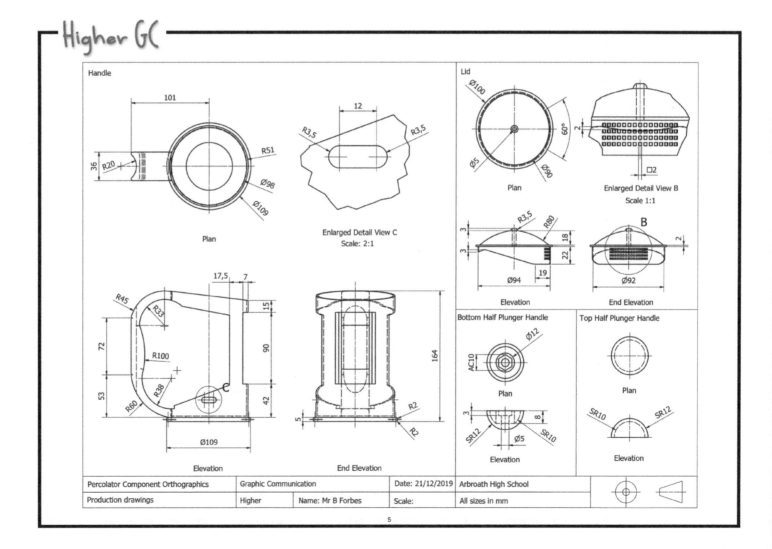

COURSEWORK

Percolator project – Assembly views

This sheet shows the orthographic assembly views asked for in this task.

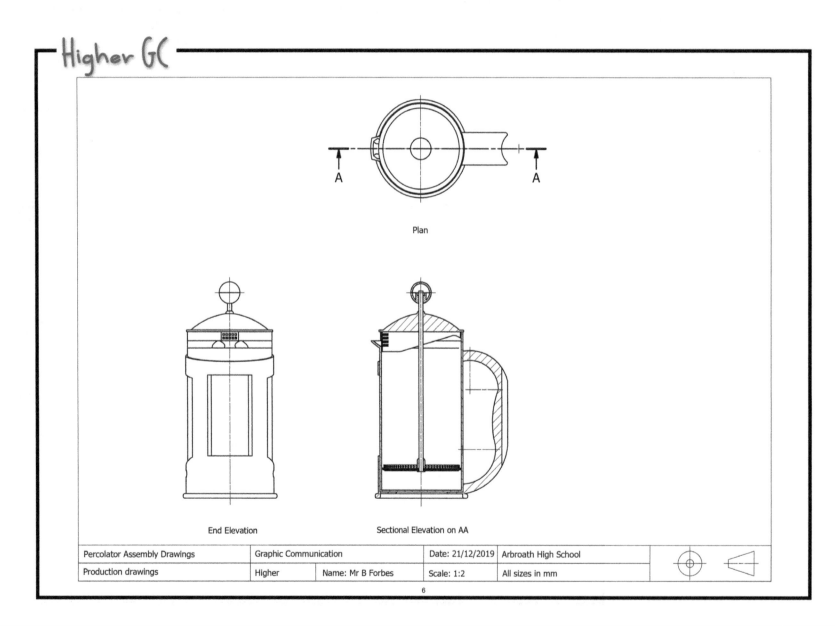

Higher GC

Plan

End Elevation

Sectional Elevation on AA

Percolator Assembly Drawings	Graphic Communication		Date: 21/12/2019	Arbroath High School
Production drawings	Higher	Name: Mr B Forbes	Scale: 1:2	All sizes in mm

6

Percolator project – Pictorial views

This task asked for an assembled isometric view and an exploded isometric view to be produced. These types of views must be produced as line drawings and not rendered or shaded.

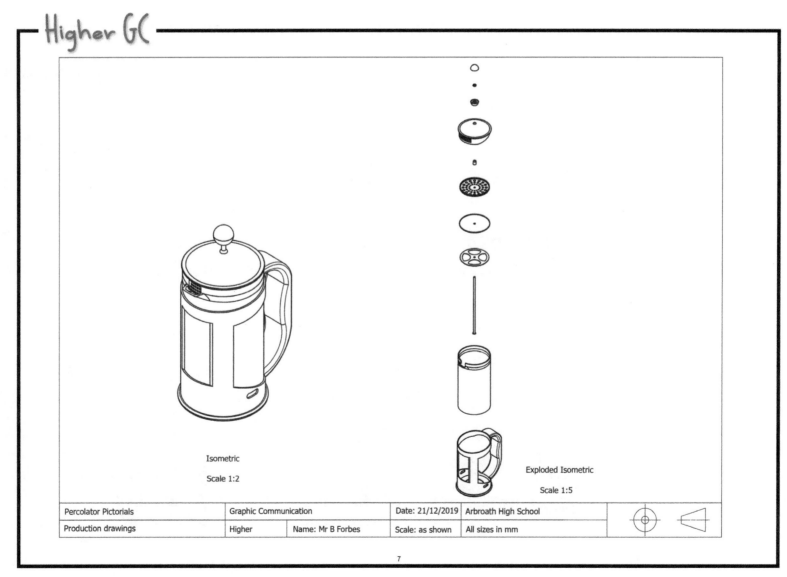

Higher GC

Isometric

Scale 1:2

Exploded Isometric

Scale 1:5

Percolator Pictorials	Graphic Communication		Date: 21/12/2019	Arbroath High School		
Production drawings	Higher	Name: Mr B Forbes	Scale: as shown	All sizes in mm		

7

Percolator project – Thumbnails

Thumbnails for both sides of the leaflet were to be produced. Six design elements/principles were to be identified at this stage.

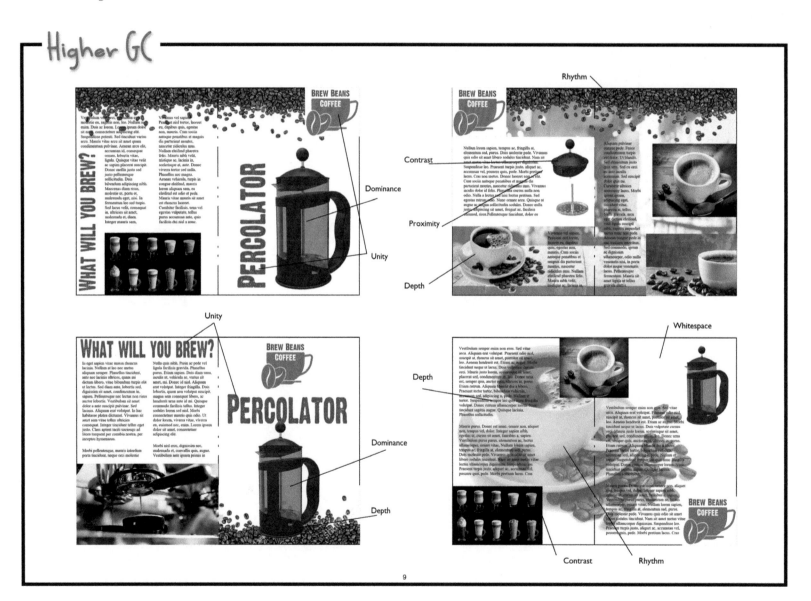

Percolator project – Final DTP leaflet

This task asked for both sides of the leaflet to be produced full size with justification for the use of six design elements and principles. This shows the other side of the leaflet.

GO! Assignment Advice

Prepare for this part of the assignment by developing a range of DTP work throughout the year. You should also develop descriptions for some of the design elements/principles ahead of the assignment. This will guarantee you marks and save time trying to word the descriptions during the assignment. Depth, dominance, unity, proximity, emphasis and contrast are all easy-to-learn stock descriptions that can be used in the assignment.

Higher GC

Line

The line is used as a column rule to help separate the columns of text to make them easier to read.

Colour

The brown has been used throughout adopting a coffee theme through matching the background to a coffee colour. The percolator is used to brew coffee so using the colour throughout helps to show this.

Unity

The repeated use of brown has been used throughout the layout to help tie it all together. This makes it obvious that all the parts are connected to the same topic. The coffee bean image at the top of the page creates a physical connection between the two pages and the opposite side of the leaflet.

WHAT WILL YOU BREW?

BREW BEANS COFFEE

PERCOLATOR

Dominance

The image of the percolator is the largest item on the page. This means that the reader will notice it first.

Proximity

The image of the percolator is positioned close to the title "Percolator". This makes it obvious that the text belongs with the image.

10

Percolator project – Final DTP leaflet

This task asked for both sides of the leaflet to be produced full size with justification for the use of six design elements and principles.

Higher GC

Contrast

A transparency has been added to contrast with the background. This makes the images and the text easier to see and read.

Depth

The coffee cup has been placed in front of the lighter strip of colour on the background image to make it stand out and appear to come toward the reader.

The glass brewer is designed to cope with boiling water for longer to allow you to brew your coffee to perfection. The handle is strong and durable.

The filter will prevent granules getting into your cup and is easy to use.

The lid fits snuggly in place without worrying if it will fall off mid pour.

Make your own barista style coffee at home without the fuss. Brew Beans percolator will produce high quality coffee for you to enjoy at home. Learn different methods of producing your favourite coffee using our percolator to relax after a day at work or to get you going in the morning.

Use Brew Beans roasted coffee with this to get the best results. We produce a variety of different tastes for your palate with some quiet, unassuming blends to hearty, fulsome coffee for those who prefer a strong cup.

This Brew Beans percolator will met all your requirements for brewing the perfect coffee every time. It is easy to clean and comes with a 5 year guarantee. If any of our parts do not meet your expectation in that time, we will replace your percolator.

This is the Brew Beans promise. Full customer satisfaction, every day.

BREW BEANS COFFEE

11

Percolator project – Rendered environment

The rendered environment is shown. The percolator has been shown on a typical kitchen worktop.

GO! **Assignment Advice**

It is likely that you will have to produce an environment as part of your assignment. Develop your skills in applying decals, materials, lighting and rendering the environment.

Higher GC

12

Tazza Lighting project

During this project you will develop your skills in producing preliminary, production and promotional graphics.

Sketching and rendering skills can be developed. If you own a tablet, you may wish to use sketching apps such as *Adobe Photoshop Sketch*® or *SketchBook – draw and paint*®. You must not use 3D CAD software to produce sketches in your assignment, therefore there is no value in using this in your coursework to produce sketches.

You will develop your 3D CAD skills throughout this project. It may be wise to use top-down modelling to ensure the parts of your lighting solution fit together.

Spend time improving your CAD rendering. This project will encourage you to add a light source emitting from the light itself.

Adding decals to a 3D CAD model is a necessary skill for your assignment. Applying this to the folding tower and ensuring that it flows around it will test your understanding.

A range of topics can be covered during this project. Comparing CMYK codes with RGB when colour is picked from an electronic copy demonstrates the importance of using CMYK codes when these are given.

You should fully justify your use of the design elements and principles. Practise describing which ones you have used, how you have used them and the effect this has had because you will have to do this in your assignment. The more you practise this, the better you will get. You will find that most of the reasons for using specific design elements and principles are the same so this can be learned during coursework and used in your assignment.

Assignment task – Tazza Lighting

Your task is to create a graphic proposal for a company called Tazza Lighting. The company is looking for a range of lighting that uses existing fixings as part of its industrial themed furniture.

Tazza Lighting has a logo and a colour scheme that must be visible throughout its advertising to help build the company brand. The logo is included in your pack as a vector graphic file. The colours used are:

CMYK code: C – 48; M –100; Y – 19; K – 4

CMYK code: C – 13; M – 0; Y – 84; K – 0.

Some of the knock-down fittings that Tazza insists you use are available as STEP files and these are also included in your assignment pack.

Tazza Lighting wants a three-fold standing advert that will accompany the lamp on a shop display. This should be no larger than A3 in size and should be able to stand independently.

You must also display the completed proposal in a suitable environment.

Your task is to produce the **preliminary, production** and **promotional** graphics required to meet the brief.

Preliminary – initial pictorial sketches

Preliminary sketches are used to give the client an idea of proposed solutions for their product. They should be rendered to a high quality to make them look realistic.

You are permitted to use electronic methods, such as a graphic sketching app, to produce these drawings. You must not use 3D CAD methods.

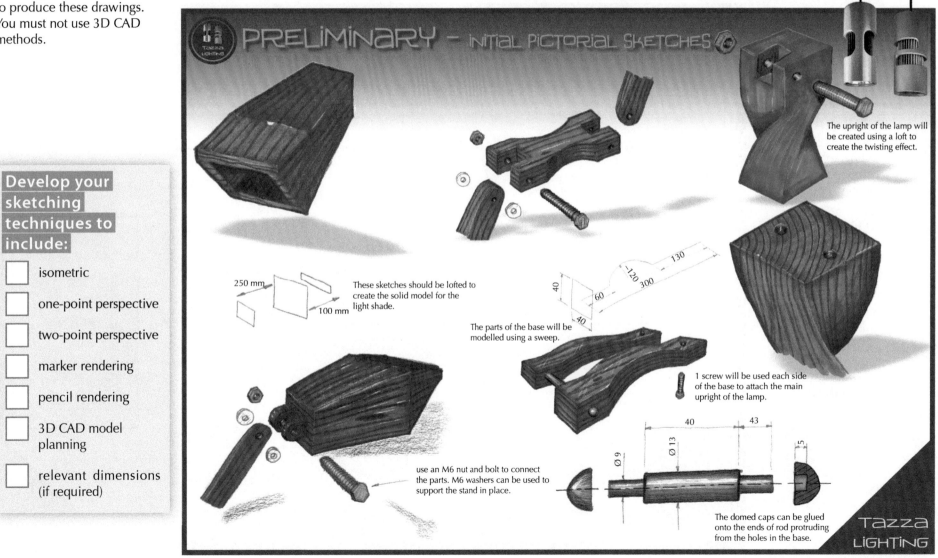

PRELIMINARY – initial Pictorial Sketches

The upright of the lamp will be created using a loft to create the twisting effect.

250 mm
100 mm
These sketches should be lofted to create the solid model for the light shade.

130
120
300
40
60
40

The parts of the base will be modelled using a sweep.

1 screw will be used each side of the base to attach the main upright of the lamp.

use an M6 nut and bolt to connect the parts. M6 washers can be used to support the stand in place.

40   43
Ø 9   Ø 13

The domed caps can be glued onto the ends of rod protruding from the holes in the base.

Tazza Lighting

Preliminary – orthographic sketches

Orthographic sketches are then developed to allow 3D CAD models of the components to be produced.

GO! **Assignment Advice**

Develop your sketching skills. Regardless of whether you use electronic methods or not, you must be able to sketch to good proportions, project views properly and provide technical detail such as centre lines and dimensions.

Develop your sketching techniques to include:

- [ ] orthographic component views of each part of the proposal

- [ ] all dimensions required to create the 3D CAD model

Make sure:

- [ ] dimensions follow British Standards 8888

- [ ] all centre lines are shown

- [ ] hidden detail, hatching lines are shown

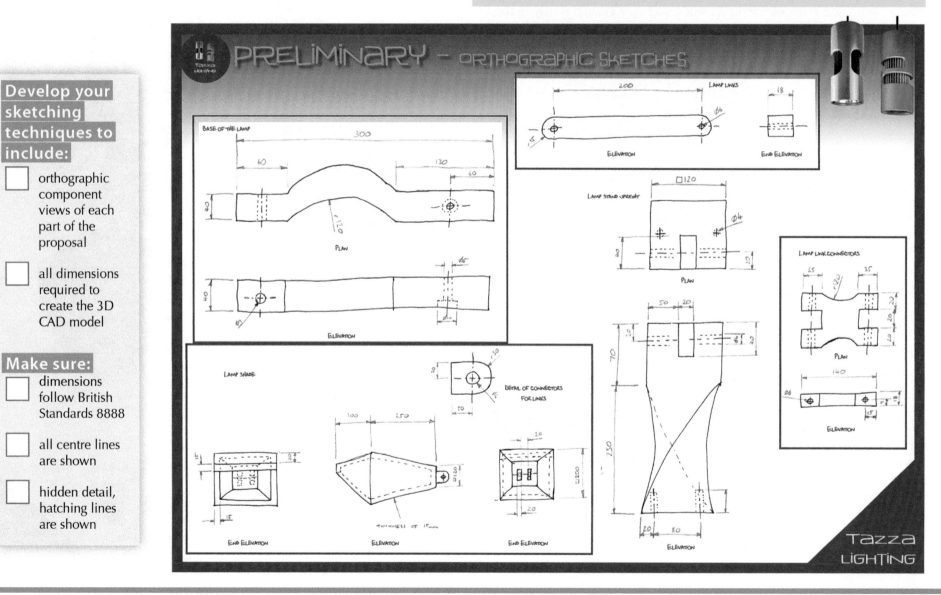

COURSEWORK

182

Preliminary – DTP planning

The DTP work must be planned in order to create a display with effective visual impact. When producing layouts and evaluating them, you must use the correct terms associated with the design elements, design principles and DTP features. It is a good idea to produce these plans using DTP software. This makes the process more efficient.

Planning

Annotations must include:

- [ ] design elements
- [ ] design principles
- [ ] DTP terms
- [ ] comments relating to the brief

All annotations must explain why the design element, design principle or DTP feature is being used.

GO! Assignment Advice

Using DTP software to produce thumbnails of your layouts in the assignment will reduce the time taken to develop these into the final version. You will also be able to use actual font styles and images to give a good idea of your intended layout.

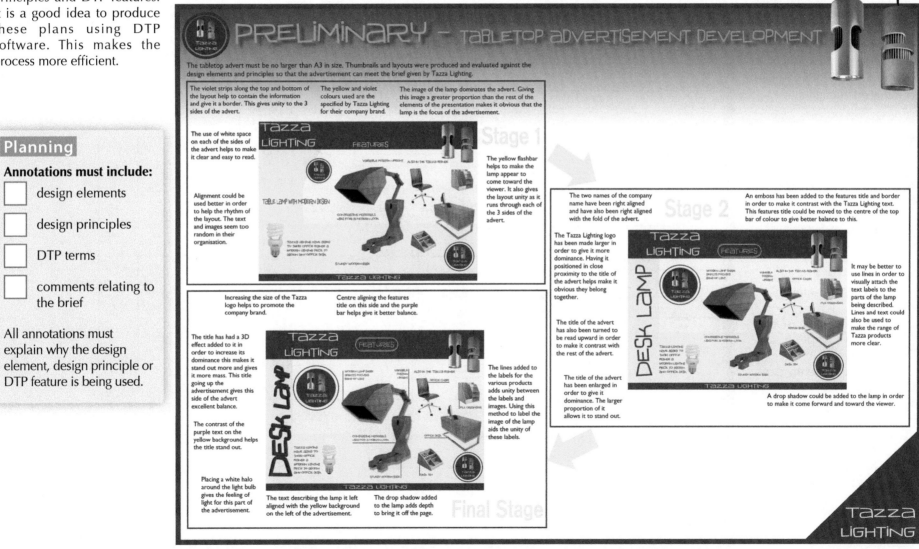

PRELIMINARY – TABLETOP ADVERTISEMENT DEVELOPMENT

The tabletop advert must be no larger than A3 in size. Thumbnails and layouts were produced and evaluated against the design elements and principles so that the advertisement can meet the brief given by Tazza Lighting.

The violet strips along the top and bottom of the layout help to contain the information and give it a border. This gives unity to the 3 sides of the advert.

The yellow and violet colours used are the specified by Tazza Lighting for their company brand.

The image of the lamp dominates the advert. Giving this image a greater proportion than the rest of the elements of the presentation makes it obvious that the lamp is the focus of the advertisement.

The use of white space on each of the sides of the advert helps to make it clear and easy to read.

Alignment could be used better in order to help the rhythm of the layout. The text and images seem too random in their organisation.

The yellow flashbar helps to make the lamp appear to come toward the viewer. It also gives the layout unity as it runs through each of the 3 sides of the advert.

The two names of the company name have been right aligned and have also been right aligned with the fold of the advert.

An emboss has been added to the features title and border in order to make it contrast with the Tazza Lighting text. This features title could be moved to the centre of the top bar of colour to give better balance to this.

The Tazza Lighting logo has been made larger in order to give it more dominance. Having it positioned in close proximity to the title of the advert helps make it obvious they belong together.

The title of the advert has also been turned to be read upward in order to make it contrast with the rest of the advert.

It may be better to use lines in order to visually attach the text labels to the parts of the lamp being described. Lines and text could also be used to make the range of Tazza products more clear.

Increasing the size of the Tazza logo helps to promote the company brand.

Centre aligning the features title on this side and the purple bar helps give it better balance.

The title has had a 3D effect added to it in order to increase its dominance this makes it stand out more and gives it more mass. This title going up the advertisement gives this side of the advert excellent balance.

The lines added to the labels for the various products adds unity between the labels and images. Using this method to label the image of the lamp aids the unity of these labels.

The title of the advert has been enlarged in order to give it dominance. The larger proportion of it allows it to stand out.

A drop shadow could be added to the lamp in order to make it come forward and toward the viewer.

The contrast of the purple text on the yellow background helps the title stand out.

Placing a white halo around the light bulb gives the feeling of light for this part of the advertisement.

The text describing the lamp it left aligned with the yellow background on the left of the advertisement.

The drop shadow added to the lamp adds depth to bring it off the page.

COURSEWORK

Production graphics – component orthographics

Use your master sheet to produce your production graphics. Separate the views of each component by drawing lines between each of the different sets of component orthographic views. Give each of the components a title.

The component production orthographic drawings must contain enough information to enable each of the parts to be manufactured. Ensure that all hidden detail, centre lines and dimensions are shown and that British Standards are followed throughout.

Develop your skills so that you can do the following:

- [ ] produce component orthographic views of all parts
- [ ] show all centre lines
- [ ] show all dimensions that would be required to be able to manufacture the parts shown
- [ ] show hidden detail
- [ ] produce title block and border with lines separating views
- [ ] follow British Standards

GO! Assignment Advice

Include enlarged detail views to show smaller parts clearly. Fully dimension each component and show all centre lines. You must ensure that you show all of the dimensions that would be required to manufacture the product. Show the dimensions given on the data sheets in the assignment to show them all.

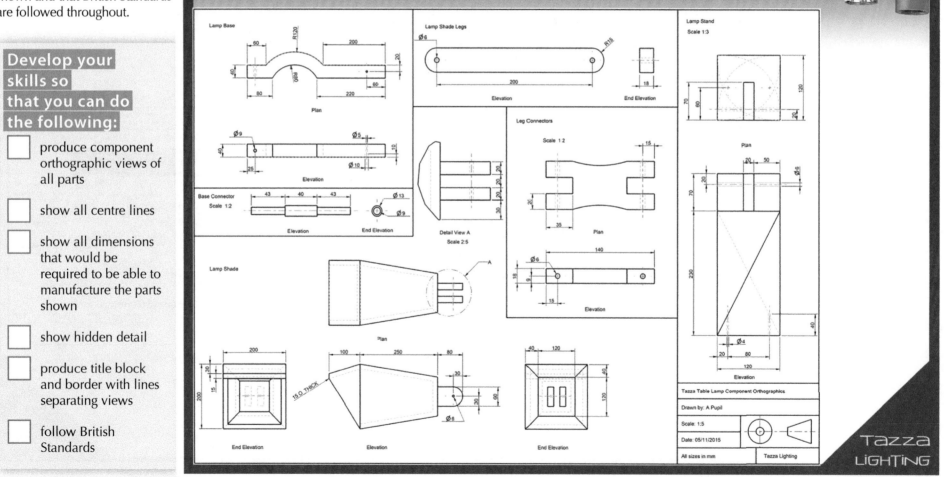

184

Production graphics – technical detail

Technical detail includes sectional views, enlarged detail views or exploded views. These types of drawing are needed to make it obvious how particular parts of a product are assembled or to show the internal construction of the parts. You need to show at least one stepped sectional view.

GO! **Assignment Advice**

Assignment Advice

Ensure you know how to produce exploded views. When you show these as part of the production drawings, do not render them. You should only show these as line drawings. For stepped sections, ensure the ends of the cutting plane face the same direction. Ensure hatching is shown only on components that require it. You must be able to remove hatching from specific areas and change the angle of it in order for it to meet British Standards.

Develop your skills so that you can do the following:

- [ ] produce a full sectional view
- [ ] produce a stepped sectional view
- [ ] produce an enlarged detail view
- [ ] produce an exploded view to show how parts are assembled
- [ ] ensure all drawing labels are correct

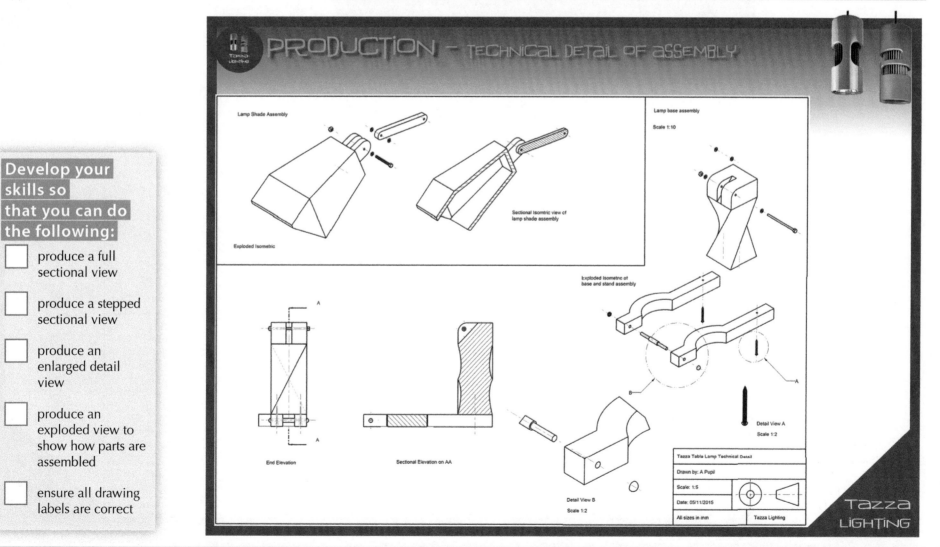

PRODUCTION – TECHNICAL DETAIL OF ASSEMBLY

Lamp Shade Assembly

Sectional Isomtric view of lamp shade assembly

Exploded Isometric

Lamp base assembly

Scale 1:10

Exploded Isometric of base and stand assembly

End Elevation

Sectional Elevation on AA

Detail View B
Scale 1:2

Detail View A
Scale 1:2

Tazza Table Lamp Technical Detail

Drawn by: A Pupil

Scale: 1:5

Date: 05/11/2015

All sizes in mm

Tazza Lighting

Tazza LIGHTING

COURSEWORK

185

Production graphics – pictorial views

You have to show pictorial views of the assembled model. You must also include exploded pictorial views on this sheet to show how the model is put together.

GO! Assignment Advice

You must show any assembled views from the same orientation as stated in the assignment. Ensure you are able to do this.

Develop your skills so that you can do the following:

- ☐ produce isometric views
- ☐ produce an exploded isometric view
- ☐ produce enlarged detail views of small parts
- ☐ ensure each view is labelled correctly

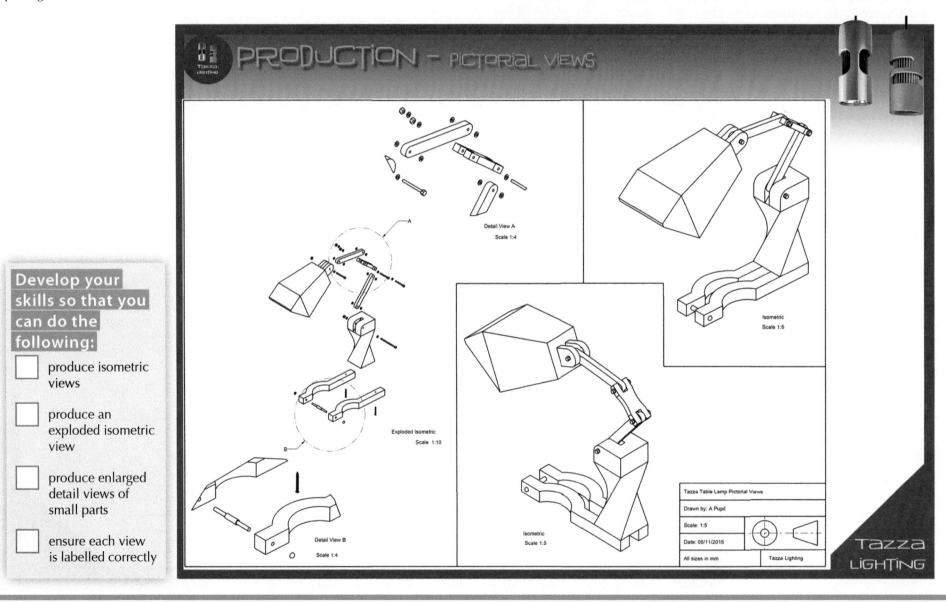

PRODUCTION – PICTORIAL VIEWS

Detail View A
Scale 1:4

Exploded Isometric
Scale 1:10

Detail View B
Scale 1:4

Isometric
Scale 1:5

Isometric
Scale 1:5

Tazza Table Lamp Pictorial Views

Drawn by: A Pupil

Scale: 1:5

Date: 05/11/2015

All sizes in mm

Tazza Lighting

Tazza Lighting

Promotional graphics – DTP work

You must be able to produce the final layout to the correct dimensions as stated in the task. You must show evidence of effective use of the design elements and the design principles. This image must be used within the environment.

(GO!) Assignment Advice

The DTP item must make excellent use of the design elements and design principles. Ensure your knowledge of these is excellent to enable you to apply them with skill. Throughout the course you should study existing layouts and graphic design textbooks such as *Go* by Chip Kidd to help generate quality layouts.

Practise using DTP software until you are confident in your ability to:

- ☐ produce layouts to the correct size
- ☐ ensure there are no spelling mistakes
- ☐ ensure all layers are in the correct order
- ☐ save your work as an image file so it can be used as a decal in the environment display

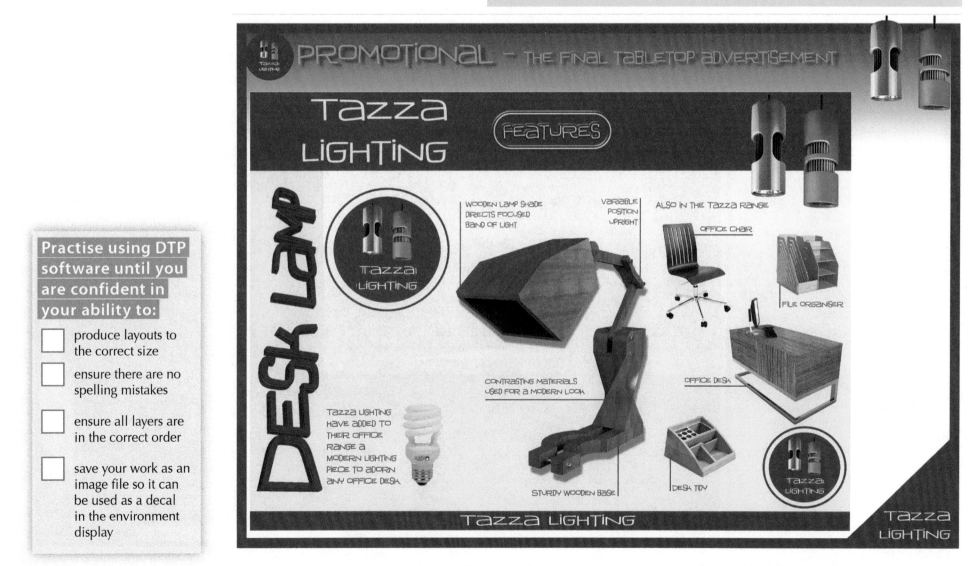

COURSEWORK

Promotional graphics – the environment

The environment will be assembled in 3D CAD and then rendered using specialist software. It must show the completed item in a relevant scene and include the DTP-produced item as a decal.

GO! Assignment Advice

The environment should include the DTP-produced item. Using specialist rendering software such as Keyshot will give the best results. Develop your skills in applying lighting techniques from specific places to improve the appearance of the environment in your assignment. The environment in your assignment should only contain the 3D CAD models given by the SQA.

Make sure that you know how to:

- [ ] show a close-up of the finished, rendered 3D model that you have produced preliminary, production and promotional graphics for

- [ ] show the DTP item you produced, displayed as a decal in the environment

- [ ] include at least two light sources in your rendered environment

- [ ] show materials, textures, shadows and reflections in your rendered scene

PROMOTIONAL – THE LAMP IN A SUITABLE ENVIRONMENT

Tazza LIGHTING

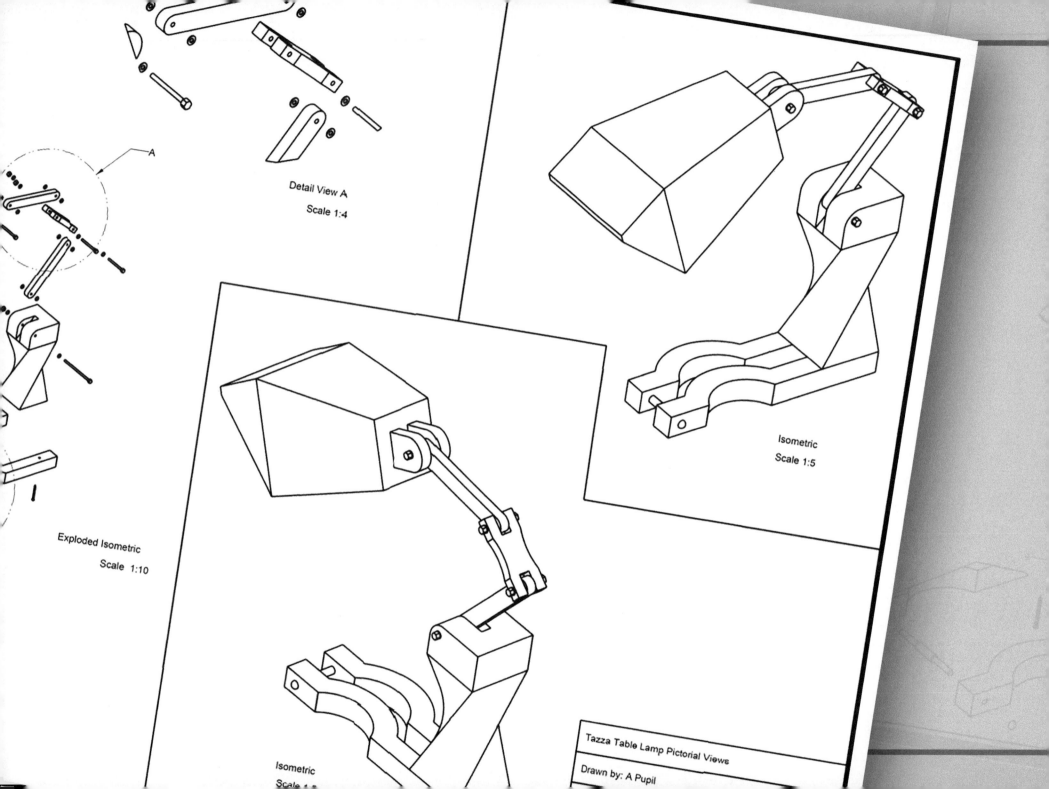

Detail View A

Scale 1:4

Exploded Isometric

Scale 1:10

Isometric

Scale 1:5

Isometric

Scale 1:

Tazza Table Lamp Pictorial Views

Drawn by: A Pupil

Chapter 9
The Assignment

You will learn

- **The assignment – Sports shaker bottle**

The assignment – Sports shaker bottle

The final assignment is worth 50 marks out of 140 overall marks in Higher Graphic Communication. You will complete the assignment under direct supervision with no assistance and no access to any external resources.

You must produce no more than ten A3 pages when meeting the requirements of the assignment.

You will have the opportunity to demonstrate your skills in the following areas:

1. preliminary graphics

2. production graphics

3. promotional graphics.

The SQA produces a new assignment every year. However, there are some areas you can practise that will help you gain the most marks possible. We will look at some of these in this section.

The assignment example shown here is not an official SQA assignment, but it does show how you could structure your assignment to gain maximum marks.

> On the SQA website there is an 'Understanding Standards' tab. This section of the website is very useful as it explains the specific reasons why marks have been allocated for pieces of work produced within assignments and exams by candidates across the country. Studying this when preparing for your assignment and exam will help you identify areas where you can develop.

Assignment preparation task – Sports shaker bottle

Task 1 – Production graphics

Create 3D CAD models of a sports shaker bottle. Use the information contained within Data sheets 1, 2 and 3. You should use your modelling plans to help you.

From these models produce:

(a) Component orthographics of the parts of the sports shaker bottle.

- Show the bottle at a scale of 1:2.
- Show the lid at a scale of 1:1.
- Show the cap at a scale of 2:1.

You must use third-angle projection. Show all hidden detail. Show suitable sectional views of each component. Show enlarged detail views where required. Show enough dimensions to allow each component to be manufactured. Produce these drawings as line drawings.

(b) Assembly orthographics of the sports shaker bottle at a scale of 1:2. You must show the plan, elevation and sectional end elevation. Ensure that the sectional end elevation shows the detail of the length of the bottle cap. You must use third-angle projection. Do not show hidden detail.

(c) An assembled isometric drawing of the sports shaker bottle at a scale of 1:1 and an exploded isometric drawing of the sports shaker bottle at a scale of 1:2. Do not show hidden detail. Produce these as line drawings with no rendering or shading.

Data sheet 1 - The Bottle

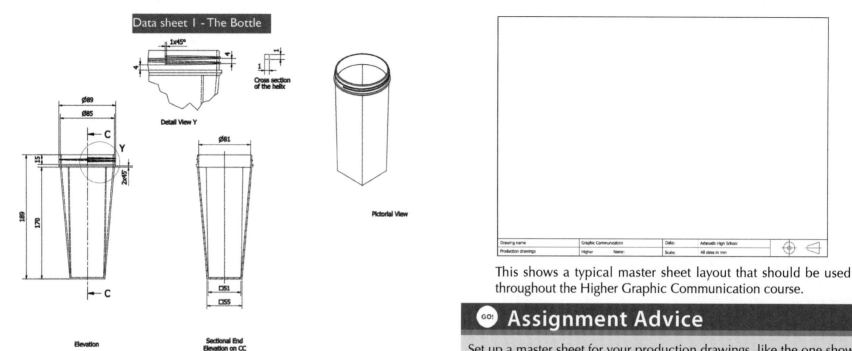

1x45°

Cross section
of the helix

Detail View Y

Ø89
Ø85

Ø81

Pictorial View

15
189
170
2x45°

C — Y

C

□51
□55

Elevation

Sectional End
Elevation on CC

This shows a typical master sheet layout that should be used throughout the Higher Graphic Communication course.

Drawing name	Graphic Communication	Date:	Arbroath High School
Production drawings	Higher Name:	Scale:	All sizes in mm

GO! Assignment Advice

Set up a master sheet for your production drawings, like the one shown, before completing the assignment tasks. Check that the third-angle projection symbol meets British Standards. Ensure that your title block does not take up a large amount of your drawing sheet. Ensure your master sheet is set up to produce views using the third-angle projection method.

Data sheet 2 - The Cap

Pictorial View

20   42

1

38

R20

Ø22

Plan

R202

10 2
2
R30

Ø26
Ø29
Ø30

Elevation

Data sheet 3 - The Lid

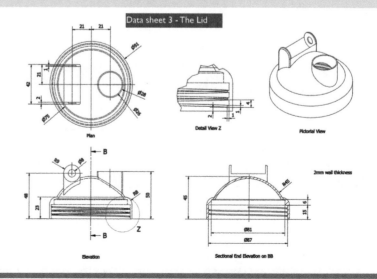

21   21

Ø91

42
21

Ø28
Ø26

Ø75

Plan

Detail View Z

Pictorial View

B

48
23

50

B
Z

Elevation

2mm wall thickness

R45

45

15 6

Ø81
Ø87

Sectional End Elevation on BB

Assignment preparation task – Sports shaker bottle

These examples show how you could lay your drawings out for Task 1. Use the scale defined in the task for each part and show these in the same orientation asked for.

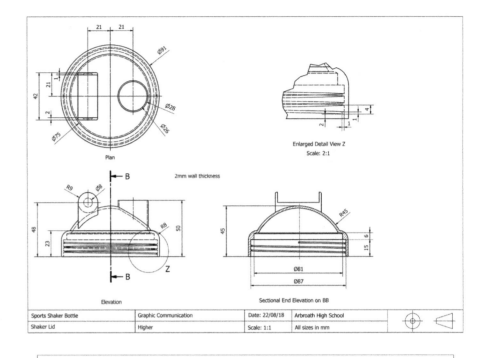

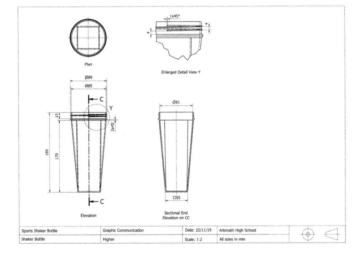

Assignment Advice

- Ensure that you include all centre lines in your production drawings.
- Include all relevant details, such as dimensions and scale in any enlarged views.
- You have to show all the necessary dimensions required to 3D CAD model the components. To do this, you will need to show all the dimensions that are given in the data sheets in the assignment task in your production drawings.

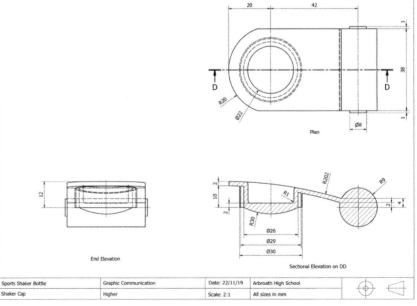

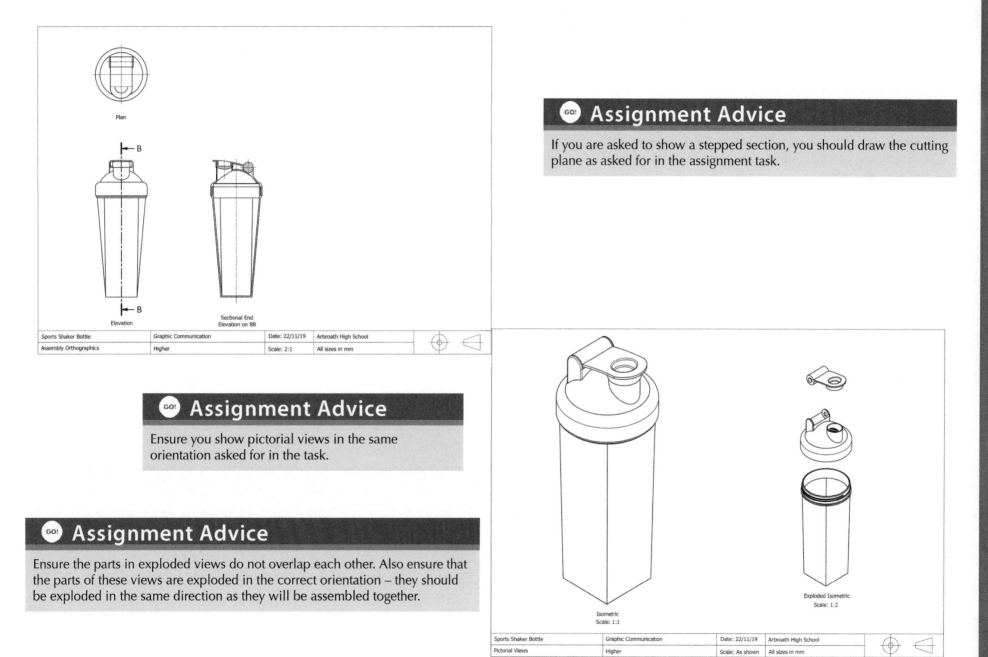

Plan

B

B

Elevation

Sectional End
Elevation on BB

| Sports Shaker Bottle | Graphic Communication | Date: 22/11/19 | Arbroath High School | | |
| Assembly Orthographics | Higher | Scale: 2:1 | All sizes in mm | | |

GO! Assignment Advice

If you are asked to show a stepped section, you should draw the cutting plane as asked for in the assignment task.

GO! Assignment Advice

Ensure you show pictorial views in the same orientation asked for in the task.

GO! Assignment Advice

Ensure the parts in exploded views do not overlap each other. Also ensure that the parts of these views are exploded in the correct orientation – they should be exploded in the same direction as they will be assembled together.

Isometric
Scale: 1:1

Exploded Isometric
Scale: 1:2

| Sports Shaker Bottle | Graphic Communication | Date: 22/11/19 | Arbroath High School | | |
| Pictorial Views | Higher | Scale: As shown | All sizes in mm | | |

THE ASSIGNMENT

195

Assignment preparation task – Sports shaker bottle

Task 2 – Promotional graphics

In order to show how the sports shaker bottle looks, you must:

(a) Create a CAD render of the assembled sports shaker bottle. All parts of the sports shaker bottle will be made from plastic with the bottle being semi-transparent and the lid and cap being opaque. Place a decal of the company logo on the bottle part of the sports shaker bottle. This image will be provided for you.

(b) In order to advertise this sports shaker bottle, you must create a layout for a promotional advert that will be used in a gym. This advert must be completed in portrait format, 1600 mm high × 1200 mm wide. Your final visual must be produced to a scale of 1:5. You must use the company colours in your promotional work. You must produce two thumbnails to help plan this advert. You have been provided with extended text and images you must use. You are not permitted to use any other text, images or items unless you have created them yourself. You must include the supplied gym logo and name, three or more images and the supplied body text in these thumbnails. You must identify six design elements and principles that you have used in each of these thumbnails.

(c) Produce a visual for this to a scale of 1:5. Fully annotate this visual, justifying why you have used your chosen six design elements and principles.

(d) The client would like to see the sports shaker bottle and the promotional layout in context.

You will be provided with a range of STEP files to help you complete this task. You must use only these STEP files and the sports shaker bottle in your environment. You must use at least five of the supplied STEP files and the assembled bottle with the decal applied in it. All parts of the environment must be CAD rendered to create a realistic scene showing material, lighting, shadows and reflections.

GO! Assignment Advice

Do not include any 3D CAD models that you did not create during the course of the assignment. You are only allowed to use the models supplied by the SQA.

Data sheet 4

These are the images that you can use when completing task 3.

You must use the gym company colours in the promotional layout:

- C 53. Y 62. M 24. K 4.
- C 83. Y 28. M 96. K 17.

The typeface to be used is **Impact** or/and **Chanson Heavy SF**.

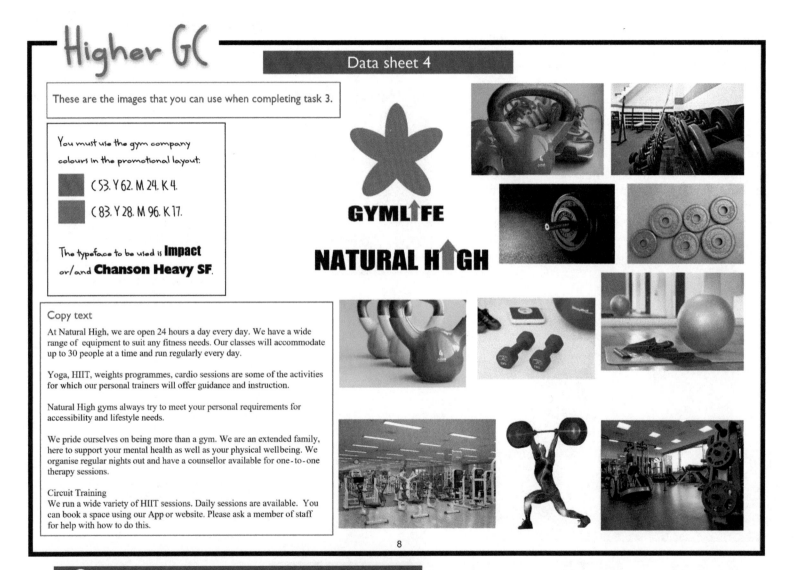

GYML**I**FE

NATURAL HIGH

Copy text

At Natural High, we are open 24 hours a day every day. We have a wide range of equipment to suit any fitness needs. Our classes will accommodate up to 30 people at a time and run regularly every day.

Yoga, HIIT, weights programmes, cardio sessions are some of the activities for which our personal trainers will offer guidance and instruction.

Natural High gyms always try to meet your personal requirements for accessibility and lifestyle needs.

We pride ourselves on being more than a gym. We are an extended family, here to support your mental health as well as your physical wellbeing. We organise regular nights out and have a counsellor available for one-to-one therapy sessions.

Circuit Training
We run a wide variety of HIIT sessions. Daily sessions are available. You can book a space using our App or website. Please ask a member of staff for help with how to do this.

8

GO! Assignment Advice

Ensure you know how to set the CMYK code in your layout. Do not colour pick the colours from the electronic version of the assignment task.

GO! Assignment Advice

Use only the graphics, extended text and typeface asked for in the assignment task.

Promotional graphics

Ensure that you complete the parts of the task exactly as asked for in the assignment. If you are asked to produce a render of the 3D CAD model with a decal applied, then this is what you should show. Ensure you show the correct materials asked for on the render.

When planning the layouts, if asked to **identify** DTP elements/principles, there is no need to **justify** them. You only need to justify if specifically asked to do so within the task. When justifying the use of design elements and principles, you should describe how they have been used and the effect this has on the layout.

When producing an environment, follow the instructions in the task. Only 3D CAD models that have been created during the assignment should be used in the environment. It is likely that the SQA will provide STEP or IGES files. It is important that you use only these along with the model you have created within the task.

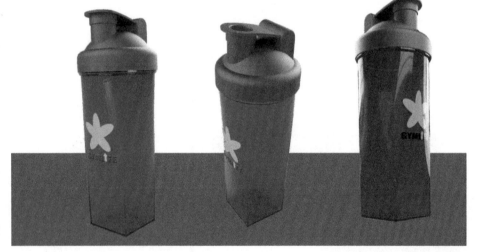

GO! Assignment Advice

Use DTP software to produce your thumbnails. This will save time when you are developing these ideas for the final visual. It will also improve the quality of the thumbnails and make your planning clearer with intended images and fonts.

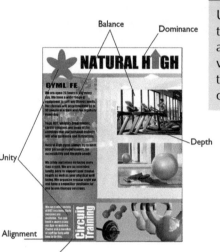

These two examples show design elements and principles being identified. Notice that this part of the task has asked for them to be identified therefore no description of their use is required in this instance.

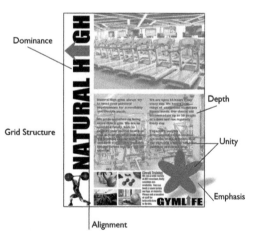

GO! Assignment Advice

You do not need to show the render of the 3D CAD model from multiple angles, but it may benefit your DTP work if you create more than one version of the rendered image.

This example shows how design elements and principles can be justified. Notice that **how** the design elements and principles have been used and the **effect** this has had on the layout have been described. When you justify your use of elements and principles in a layout, ensure you comment on both of these areas.

Dominance - the Gymlife logo is the largest element on the page in order that it stands out and is noticed first.

Depth - images placed onto a transparency in order to help them stand out. Having them in front of other elements will allow them to appear to come forward as they are in the front of the layout.

Balance - the left-hand side of the layout contains mainly text while the right-hand side of the layout consists mainly of images. This balances the layout as the heavier images can allow the text to play a clear role and help people read it.

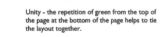

Alignment - the left-hand sides of the images and the caption are left aligned. This keeps this part of the layout organised and easy to follow down the page and clearly links the text with the images.

Line - lines are used either side of the headings for the circuit training area in order to help make the headings stand out and to better organise the extended text. This makes the extended text easier to read by giving the reader a clear structure to this part of the layout.

Unity - the repetition of green from the top of the page at the bottom of the page helps to tie the layout together.

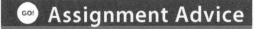

Assignment preparation task – Sports shaker bottle

Task 3 – Preliminary graphics

The company is looking to create a range of products to enhance the gym experience for its users.

One product the company is currently looking at developing is shelving for toiletries in the showers.

The shelf holder is to be made from stainless steel and the shelf is to be made from acrylic.

Using the drawings on data sheet 5, you must:

(a) Produce orthographic component sketches of the elevation, plan and end elevation of the various parts of the shelf unit. You must show all hidden detail in your sketches and use third-angle projection.

(b) Produce rendered orthographic sketches of the assembled shelf unit. You should use marker pens and colour pencils as the render media.

(c) Produce a rendered pictorial assembly sketch of the shelf unit.

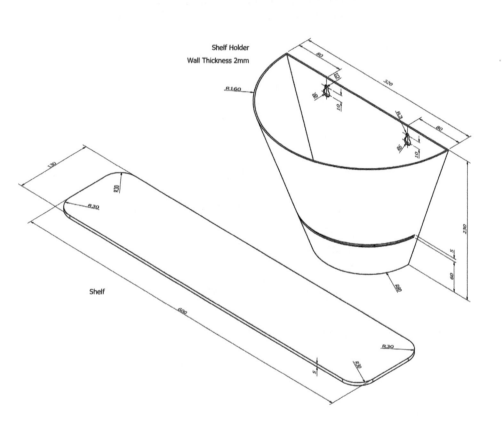

Shelf Holder
Wall Thickness 2mm

Shelf

SHELF HOLDER

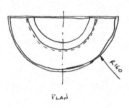

PLAN

SHELF

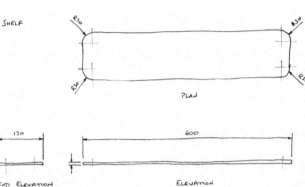

PLAN

130

600

END ELEVATION

ELEVATION

Assignment Advice

Ensure sketches are shown in third-angle projection, produced to good proportions and show all dimensions required to 3D CAD model the parts.

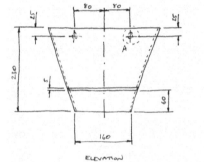

ELEVATION

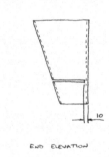

END ELEVATION

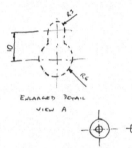

ENLARGED DETAIL
VIEW A

Assignment Advice

You must not use any form of 3D CAD modelling software when completing sketching tasks.

PLAN

ELEVATION

END ELEVATION

THE ASSIGNMENT

201

BUZZ SPORT POWERS YOU

BETTER THAN THE REST

Here at Buzz Sport, we know that power doesn't come from determination alone. Pep talks and motivational speeches can only go so far.

Why not trust the experts at Buzz Sport and try our new drink that has been scientifically proven to provide more power than any other competing product? Power, strength and endurance can increase by over 25% – it's a fact! Grab a bottle and see the results for yourself.

Do you feel the BUZZ?

Trusted

Chapter 10

Exam Questions

You will learn

- **The exam**
- **Digital advertising**
- **DTP printing techniques**
- **DTP – types of images**
- **The 3 Ps**
- **Tolerances questions**
- **Assignment advice**

Throughout this book there have been helpful hints for you to follow that will help you to successfully answer the exam questions and gain an excellent mark.

This part of the book will provide some help on how to structure your answers to typical exam questions. For some questions, you will be able to memorise the responses in this section to give you a helping hand in your exam. Some types of questions will appear every year. Having answers prepared for these types of questions will improve your mark and overall grade.

3D CAD exam questions

3D CAD questions will definitely be a key feature of the exam. You will be asked to describe how to carry out the following 3D CAD functions: extrude, revolve, extrude along a path, lofting and creating a helix. Make sure you use the key words described in the 3D CAD section of this book. These are highlighted in bold in the exemplar answers shown here.

You should also ensure that you use sketches to support your answer. The question will say that you may use sketches to support your answer. Read this as you **will** use sketches to support your answer. These do not have to be works of art, but must clearly indicate what you describe in your answer. Answering 3D CAD questions in this way will help you gain the marks available for these types of questions.

Sample 3D CAD exam question

A fashion company is looking to launch a range of new fragrances to complement its clothes. Drawings for a bottle for the fragrance have been developed, but they now have to be created in CAD.

Describe how the CAD technician could create a 3D CAD model of the fragrance bottle. You may use sketches to support your answer.

GO! Exam Tip

When answering 3D CAD modelling questions, you must make reference to some keywords. In this example these have been highlighted in bold. Underlining them in your exam will help you ensure you use these words.

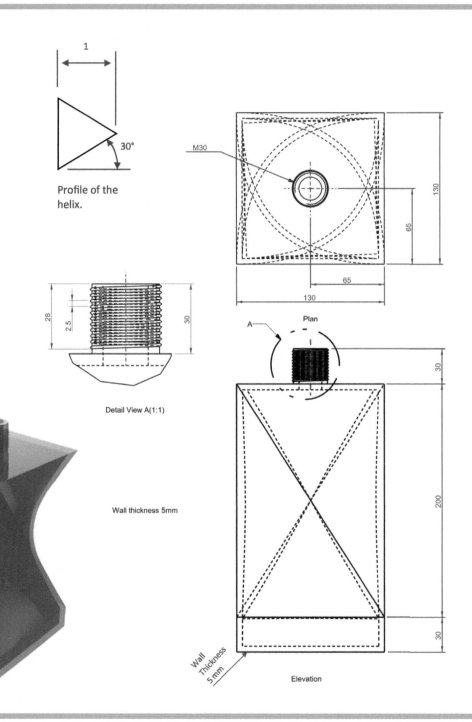

Profile of the helix.

Detail View A(1:1)

Wall thickness 5mm

Plan

Elevation

Wall Thickness 5 mm

Step 1

Sketch the **profile** of the base of the bottle.

130

130

Step 2

Extrude this profile by 30 mm to add material.

30

Step 3

To create the **loft** for the bottle, two sketches are needed. First, sketch a profile of 130 × 130 mm on top of the solid for the base.

130

130

Step 4

Create a new **workplane** 200 mm above the top of the sketch just drawn.

200

Step 5

Sketch the **profile** of the top of the bottle on this new workplane. This should be positioned directly above the original sketch.

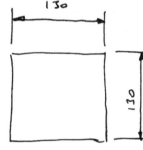

130

130

Step 6

Create a **loft** between the two sketches. This **loft** path must contain a twist, so start at one point on the bottom sketch and finish at the next point on the top sketch.

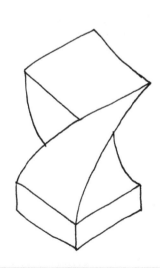

Step 7

For the top of the bottle, create a **profile** by sketching on the top face of the solid.

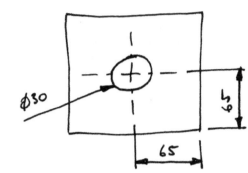

Step 8

Extrude this profile upward by 30 mm to add material.

Step 9

Shell the solid to give a wall thickness of 5 mm. Select the top face of the bottle to open this.

Step 10

Create a **workplane** that passes through the centre of the bottle. This will be positioned 65 mm from the side of the bottle.

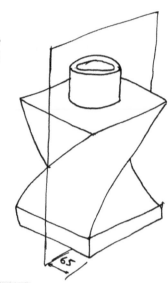

Step 11

Onto this workplane, sketch the **profile** of the **helix**. Included in this sketch will be the **centre axis** and the offset distance. For clarity, the profile and centre axis have been labelled in this answer. You may also wish to do this.

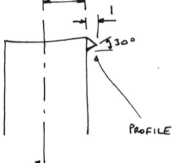

Step 12

Use the **helix** command to create the helix. Define the **pitch** to be 2.5 mm. The **length of the helix** should be 28 mm.

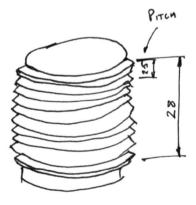

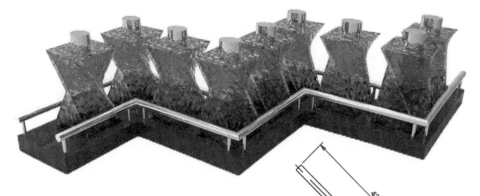

The perfume bottle is shown as it would be displayed on its display rack in a shop.

The rack is to be modelled using 3D CAD. Describe how the CAD technician would produce the rail of the rack.

Step 1

Create a sketch of the **profile** of the rail.

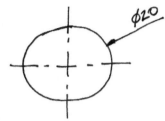

Step 2

On a separate sketch, create the **path** for the solid to be created using the **extrude along a path** command.

Step 3

Use the **extrude along a path** command to create the model, adding material. Select the circle as the **profile** and the line as the **path**.

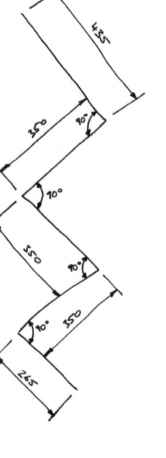

Plan

3D CAD features

To help prepare for your exam, you should practise how to structure your answers.

You should learn the number of steps required for each of the 3D CAD modelling techniques before sitting the exam. Writing down these steps will help you to structure your answer.

Repeating your thought process for these type of questions will help improve your study and exam performance. One way of doing this is by going through each of the commands in order and asking yourself if you can use each to model the drawings shown.

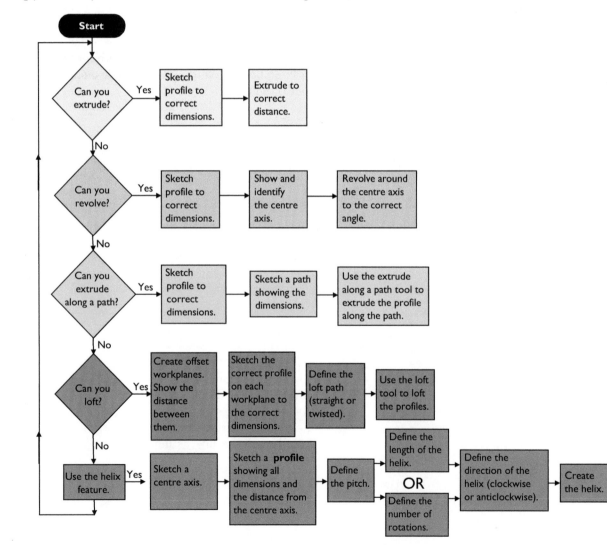

3D CAD edits

You can also prepare for the exam in the same way for the 3D CAD modelling edits that you need to know.

Learn the key words that are used and repeat them each time you are asked these questions, ensuring that you state dimensions used and include sketches where appropriate. Follow the steps shown here and repeat this each time for success in your exam.

Preparing and practising this will help you. You will then be able to repeat the wording of your answer each time. The only real changes will be to the sketches you use in your answers. The sketches will show profiles and edits where using words would be too confusing.

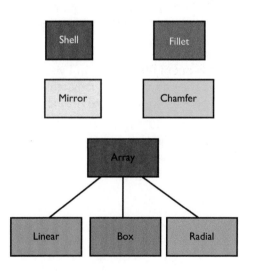

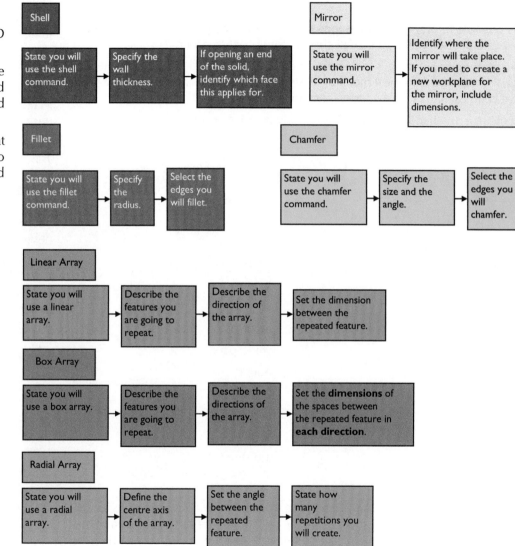

DTP questions

It is possible to prepare for questions based on desktop publishing, even though the example used in the exam will change from paper to paper.

The most important thing is to know the design elements and design principles for a DTP document. You must mention these in your answers and explain how they have been used to assist the appearance of the publication.

There are a number of common features to look out for within any presentation.

The Design Elements

line

mass/weight

shape

size

texture

colour

The Design Principles

alignment

balance

contrast

depth

dominance

unity

proximity

white space

proportion

rhythm

emphasis

value

grid structure

Colour is the most basic design element, so try to comment on the reasons for the colour choice. Refer to the properties of the colour and the feelings and emotions that are associated with it. If accent colours are used, it is normally to provide unity and rhythm.

Alignment is often used to add structure to a DTP layout so that it is easier to follow and looks visually organised. When describing alignment, you must mention two or more parts of the layout that have been aligned and the type of alignment that has been used.

White space does not have to be areas of white – it can be areas of colour without any text or images.

Large parts of the layout can use proportion to create emphasis. Drop shadows are also often used to create emphasis.

Make sure you name the design element or design principle that you are referring to in each part of your answer.

The question will ask you to answer it according to the design elements and design principles, so in order to gain the marks, you must mention them in your answer. A good tip here is to start each point by stating the design element or design principle you are describing.

Your exam is positively marked, which means that if the question is asking for five points (it is out of five marks) and you make more than five points, you will not lose marks. You can make as many references to design elements and design principles as you like, so, if you are unsure about an answer, make as many points as you can.

You can see in the exemplar exam question on the right, that many more points have been made than are required for the six marks available. You will not have correct answers cancelled out by wrong ones by answering questions in this way.

Describe how the advertisement on the right has used the design elements and design principles to convey the key information about the product being advertised.

(6 marks)

Shape – a rectangle has been used to create a border for the text and images. This forms a frame to contain all of the images and body text on the poster and keep them together.

Colour – accent colours have been used throughout the poster. These colours have been colour picked from the bottle. This helps with the rhythm of the poster as it is obvious that the various parts belong together.

Colour – the lighter tone of green used around the athletes helps to make this part of the poster dominant. The gradient fill becoming darker toward the outside gives good rhythm to the advertisement, guiding the reader's eye from the dominant image to the edges of the poster.

Mass/weight – the image of the athletes has greater mass than the area of text on the left. This gives balance to the advertisement and means the lengthy area of text is more likely to be read.

Contrast – the green, pink and white contrast so that the text stands out against the background. The white text contrasts with the dark background to give it emphasis. The title is placed on a pink background to create contrast with the rest of the poster to help it stand out.

Contrast – reverse text is used for the title and subtitles to make them stand out from the body text. Drop shadows have been applied to these titles and subtitles to create further emphasis.

Contrast – the white line and background for the text on the bottom-right of the poster contrast with the bottle. The bottle being placed in front of this area helps it to come forward and create emphasis in the poster. The white rectangle here acts as a flashbar.

Depth – the image of the bottle is placed on a layer in front of the image of the athletes. The athletes are placed on a layer that overlaps the white box to bring this image toward the reader. Drop shadows have been applied to the pink boxes to bring them forward toward the reader.

Alignment – the body text, heading and tagline are left aligned with each other. This helps with the structure of the text, guiding the reader from one part down to the next.

Proportion – the large image dominates the poster. As the next largest items, the titles are then read, which leads you onto the smaller body text, creating **rhythm**. As the bottle is also large in size, it is quickly noticed by the reader.

Proximity/unity – the bottle being positioned close to the large image makes this the focal point of the poster. It creates a connection between the product and the successful athletes.

White space – the areas to the left of the poster are left clear so that the poster is not too crowded and to allow the reader breathing space. It helps to give the main parts of the poster visual impact.

Digital advertising

You are likely to be asked questions about digital methods of advertising. These questions will ask you about the advantages of using this method of advertising for both the consumer and the producer and also the environmental impact of using this type of advertising. Digital advertising can be defined as any sort of advertisement that occurs on a digital device, whether that be a large digital display, a phone, a tablet or a computer.

You must not answer this question with 'it is easier', 'it is cheaper' or 'it is quicker'. You must quantify these answers to state exactly what may be easier or quicker.

Advantages for the consumer include:

- Digital advertising can incorporate videos which are embedded into an advert or related article. This can allow the user to better understand the purpose of a product and how to use it.
- The user can view digital publications across a range of devices, at home and when out and about and even in the dark.
- Many people use social media and will be able to easily share adverts they think friends will find interesting using these platforms.
- Links to websites can be embedded into articles and adverts, allowing the user to go directly to the company's website for more information or to purchase the product.
- The user does not have to go to a shop to buy a magazine as they can download it directly to their device.
- It is easy to zoom into small details in an image or to make small text sizes easier to read.

There are also advantages for the advertising company. These include:

- Adverts can be placed directly onto social media platforms and other websites, enabling them to reach a larger and more targeted audience.
- Electronic billboards can be updated immediately with limited costs and environmental impacts as there is no need to reprint the advert or for someone to use fuel driving to the billboard to put the poster up.
- Changes can be made to adverts without the financial and environmental cost of reprinting and redistributing.

- People can share articles/adverts they find interesting through social media, which increases the potential audience for no increased cost.
- Adverts can be easily translated into different languages or adapted to target particular audiences.
- It is better for the environment because resources like ink and paper are not needed.
- A range of adverts for different products can be shown in a single electronic billboard, which potentially increases advertising revenue for that space and for the individual advertisers. The changing images are more eye catching and should attract more attention than a static printed billboard.
- Videos displaying the product being used can be embedded into adverts which can make the product more attractive to the user.
- As digital adverts are often linked to the website of the company selling the product, people can instantly make purchases or carry out further research into the product, increasing the chance of a sale.
- Newspapers and magazines can publish targeted articles through social media. Their advertising revenue may then increase because of the greater number of readers of their publication.

Some disadvantages of digital advertising are:

- Printing companies may struggle to survive, causing job losses in this industry.
- Openly shared digital information can be easy to copy, which creates copyright issues.
- Only people with digital devices can view digital adverts, which can reduce the potential market.
- Digital publications can only be viewed where there is access to the Internet.
- Many users still prefer a paper product.
- Printed copies can be left where a range of people can access them; for example, in waiting rooms or on passenger aircraft.

🔵 Exam Tip

Learn three points from each of these areas to help you answer this type of question. Ensure that you quantify your answers and relate them to the exam question being asked.

It is likely that you will be asked to demonstrate your understanding of DTP pre-press and printing techniques. Within this, you may be asked about registration marks, crop marks and image types.

Registration marks allow the accuracy of the printing alignment of the CMYK colours to be checked. This is an important part of the printing process to prevent expensive print runs with mistakes. If the printing heads are not aligned correctly, then images will appear blurry.

These are two examples of registration marks that can be used.

Crop marks show where the pages are trimmed by a machine in order to cut the pages of a publication to the required size. These are particularly helpful when there are bleed images. Any images or part of a presentation that are to extend to the edges of the page will have to be printed beyond these crop marks to ensure accuracy when trimmed.

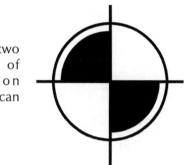

🔘 Exam Tip

Registration marks allow the CMYK printing alignment to be checked. Crop marks show where the paper should be trimmed after printing.

🔘 Exam Tip

You must know the difference between raster and vector images and you must be able to describe where each should be used.

A range of image types can be used when producing a DTP document. You will be required to demonstrate an understanding of these in your exam. Two of the most popular types are vector and raster images.

Vector files will predominantly be used where the image needs to be resized without loss of quality. Solid colour fills within vector images (for lines, shapes and text) can be easily edited within DTP software.

Raster images will be used where photographs are part of a layout. The file size for raster graphics depends on where they are being used. If the graphic is to be hosted on an Internet page, then its file size will be made smaller, 72 ppi to 96 ppi, to allow the page to load quickly. If the raster image is to be printed, then it will be produced to a much higher quality, no smaller than 300 ppi.

Raster images can become pixelated when increased in size and are therefore less suited for large-size print projects. When raster images are produced to large dimensions with large amounts of detail, they will have a large file size. Very complex raster images are difficult to convert to vector images.

Vector images will be used where a large image is required as they can be resized to far larger dimensions without any pixilation. Vector files can have a smaller file size than a raster file, which makes them ideal for websites as they load quickly. It is easy to edit the colours of the various parts of a vector file (background, line, text) in DTP software. Clear and precise graphics can be produced. Vector files are especially suited to drawings and illustrations, company logos and technical drawings. Transparency can easily be applied to a background, which makes a vector file ideal for being used in DTP software or as a decal to be printed onto a product. When manufacturing, vector files can be used to inform the path of a laser cutter.

Raster image showing tonal change.

Vector image showing tonal change.

Vector graphics are not suitable for images with gradual tonal changes with blended colour. Only specialised software packages can be used to create these type of graphics.

Two images are shown here. The image on the top is far more complex than the one on the bottom. If both of these images were vector files then the image on the top would have a much larger file size than that of the image on the bottom. In contrast to this, if these were raster or bitmap images, they would have the same file size. This is why raster files tend to be used to display images on the Internet.

The 3 Ps

You may be asked about the types of graphics produced in the 3 Ps. It can be advantageous to learn some small phrases that you can use to answer such questions.

Preliminary

These are initial sketches that give the client an idea of what the graphic proposal will look like. Preliminary graphics can be produced using either manual or digital techniques.

They will also be used to inform the development of the CAD drawings.

Using digital techniques can allow real materials to be added to sketches and can allow the client to give higher-quality feedback than some manual sketches allow.

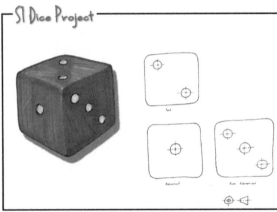

Production

These are high-quality, CAD-produced, fully dimensioned graphics that will allow manufacture. These can include: sectional views, enlarged views, cutaway views, exploded views, assemblies and component views.

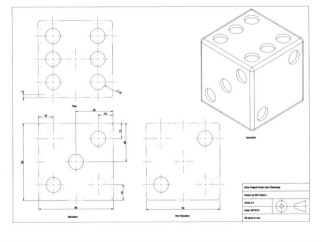

Promotional

These are computer produced, fully rendered graphics that will advertise the product. These often show the product in context for consumers and will contain some advertising material produced using DTP methods.

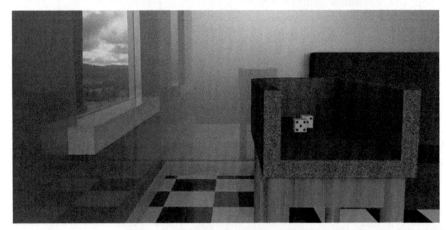

Questions about tolerances are often asked in a similar way to the method shown here. It is common for you to be tested on your knowledge of the range of methods of tolerancing and your ability to work out the range of dimensions within the context of a question.

A fence post and gate post are shown in the drawing below.

State the minimum and maximum size X is allowed to be.

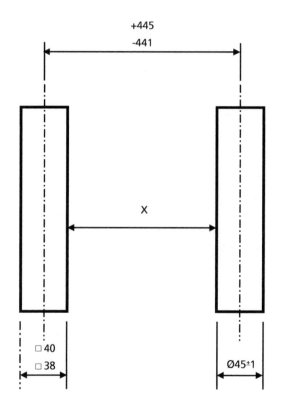

Minimum size for X

To find this, you need to use the smallest distance between the centres of the two posts. Follow this by finding the largest possible widths for the posts. In this example, you would have to remember to halve the widths of the posts.

$$441 - 20 - 23 = \underline{398}$$

Maximum size for X

To find this, you need to use the largest distance between the centres of the two posts. Follow this by finding the smallest possible widths of the posts. In this example, you would have to remember to halve the widths of the posts.

$$445 - 19 - 22 = \underline{404}$$

Exam Tip

You should take a calculator into your exam to ensure no mistakes are made if you are asked to carry out calculations.

Assignment advice

Preliminary work

It is important to develop your skills in sketching, rendering and producing DTP development work (thumbnails) throughout the course. Online tutorials can help you to produce pictorial sketches. YouTube, for example, has a wide range of resources that can help, such as *The Design Sketchbook* or *Sketch-a-Day by Spencer Nugent* channels, which will help you develop your sketching and rendering skills.

Use marker pens and pencils to create renders. Practise your technique by watching online tutorials and spending time working on these skills. Use bleed-proof paper and a range of soft and hard pencils. Practise makes perfect, so keep developing your skills throughout the year.

You will notice from your coursework and online tutorials that some graphic artists use a stylus pen and a tablet for electronic sketching. Packages such as Autodesk SketchBook or Adobe Photoshop Sketch are modern methods of producing manual sketches that allow these sketches to be easily included in promotional work if required. In your assignment, it is acceptable to use electronic sketching methods. These methods would include using a graphics tablet or a tablet with apps installed and a stylus pen. However, you must not use 3D CAD software to produce any work to be sketched in the assignment. In addition to this, it would not be acceptable to produce work for this area using 3D CAD software then change the line types using vector graphics software. For any sketching-based task in the assignment, the SQA instructions state, 'If an electronic method is used it must not be 3D CAD software (candidates will gain no marks if this software is used)'.

Production drawings

Set up a master sheet for your production drawings ahead of the assignment. You should ideally set this up at the beginning of the course and use it for all your production work.

The master sheet should be an A3 page set up to complete your work in third-angle projection. Ensure the title block on this sheet doesn't take up too much of the page.

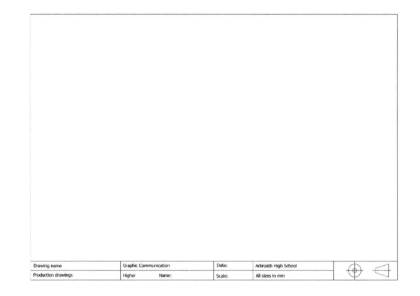

Drawing name	Graphic Communication	Date:	Arbroath High School	
Production drawings	Higher Name:	Scale:	All sizes in mm	

Once you have completed the 3D CAD models, you will need to produce the production graphics. Add all required centre lines first, then the dimensions. When adding dimensions, look closely at the data sheets. If a dimension is shown on the data sheet, ensure you include it on your graphic. If you see centre lines on the data sheets, then ensure you show these in your graphics too. Produce the views to the scale specified in the assignment.

Promotional work

You should develop your skills in producing DTP layouts by working on a range of layouts for various products and contexts throughout the year. This will give you a good base knowledge for the assignment when you will be under time constraints and have no access to other resources.

Your teacher will guide you during the year to develop your DTP work and there are a number of graphic design textbooks that you will almost certainly use in school. Books like *Graphic Design For Everyone* by Cath Caldwell and *GO: A Kidd's Guide to Graphic Design* will help you understand some of the basics of layout techniques, which will help you in your assignment.

You will have to produce the DTP work to the correct size. Ensure you know how to set shapes or pages to exact sizes.

It is likely that as part of your assignment you will have to justify the use of a range of design elements/principles. You can prepare for this before the assignment begins by learning why particular design elements/principles are used. You will then simply need to relate these reasons to the work you have produced for the assignment task. For example:

Dominance

The _____ is the largest item in the layout. This creates dominance for the _____ by ensuring it is the first item noticed by the viewer.

Unity

The repeated use of the [colour, shape, font] on the _____ creates unity. This makes it obvious that these parts of the layout belong together. This ties the layout together and helps the reader understand the information the layout is giving.

Depth

The layers of the layout ensure that the _____ is in front of the_____ in the DTP work. Due to the _____ being in front of the other parts, this means that it appears to come forward off the page toward the viewer. This draws the viewer's attention to the _____ that is being advertised.

Contrast

The _____ and the _____ are different [colours, shapes, sizes, fonts] to create contrast. This makes the _____ stand out so that the reader can see this clearly.

Proximity

The_____ and the _____ in the layout are positioned close to each other, which creates proximity. This makes it clear to the reader that they belong with one another.

Emphasis

A [drop shadow, glow, etc.] has been applied to the _____. This creates emphasis by drawing attention to the _____ and helping the reader see this by making it stand out in the layout.

Architectural drawings

At Higher level, you may be asked about some of the details found in the drawings used when developing land and buildings. These questions are likely to ask about the type of details found in these drawings.

Floor Plans – scale 1:50

- north symbol
- material contained within walls, such as insulation or brickwork
- plumbing and electrical fittings
- furniture and flooring layout
- building features, such as stairs, windows, doors, garage doors

Site Plans – scale 1:200

- the size and position of a building and its boundary area to scale
- the north symbol, to show the direction that the building and other features are facing
- contour lines
- trees: shown in position; to be removed; or proposed trees
- the position of drainage and amenities, such as gas, electrical and water supplies

Location Plans – scale 1:1250

- north symbol, to allow the plan to be read properly in relation to a map
- the size of a building and surrounding area to scale
- location of building and surrounding streets and buildings
- any geographical details that would be found on an OS map, such as contour lines, rivers, woodland, footpaths, railways, bridges, lakes

CAD library

You should memorise a short passage in order to answer questions on what a CAD library or a library of stock CAD models is and why they are used.

You can use a passage similar to the one below:

A CAD library is a collection of commonly used components, which can be placed in a drawing without the need for redrawing them each time. This saves the CAD technician time when producing drawings.

CAD libraries can be used to store 3D CAD models (which can be used within projects) or to store building symbols for use in architectural drawings. Library symbols can be drawn to British Standards to allow standardisation of parts and components.

CAD file formats

STEP/IGES files are a universal file type for use with 3D CAD models. This means that STEP/IGES files can be opened by any 3D CAD software package. One advantage of using STEP/IGES file types is seen when working with an online 3D CAD library. When accessing files from the 3D CAD library, using a STEP or IGES file means that, regardless of the type of software package being used, these types of models can be opened when building an environment.

Modelling tree

The modelling tree is the list of commands that have been used to 3D CAD model a component. This allows the user to easily identify any command or sketch that needs to be edited. The user can also reorder some of the commands to edit the model.

Model × + Q ≡
- top of bottle
  - Solid Bodies(1)
  - View: Master
  - Origin
  - Revolution1
  - Fillet1
  - Shell1
  - Work Plane3
  - Extrusion3
  - Work Plane1
  - Extrusion1
  - Extrusion2
  - Work Plane2
  - Extrusion4
  - Extrusion5
  - Work Plane4
  - Extrusion6
  - Extrusion7
  - Extrusion8
  - Fillet2
  - Coil1
  - Chamfer1
  - End of Part

Cloud computing

Some 3D CAD programs are cloud based. This means that the program doesn't take up storage space on the user's PC or laptop. This allows less-powerful computers to run the software because most of the features of the software that require a lot of power or RAM, such as the rendering process, will be done in the cloud rather than on the user's computer.

Cloud storage provides large amounts of storage space for free or a small cost and allows the user to set up their account to automatically upload their files to act as backup copies. These files can then be accessed from anywhere in the world via an Internet connection.

The biggest disadvantage of cloud computing is the need for a reliable Internet connection. Without Internet access, it is impossible to access any files stored in the cloud or to run any cloud-based CAD packages.

Digital sketching

Using a tablet and a stylus to produce sketches electronically has a number of advantages. You may be asked about these in your exam. Some of these advantages are listed below.

Sketches can be completed in layers, which helps with later editing work. Electronic sketches can be exported into other programs, such as DTP software, in order to enhance their appearance for showing a client. These sketches can be automatically saved to a cloud account so they are easy to share and are less likely to be lost through memory being wiped. Electronic sketches do not need to be scanned for sharing electronically; therefore, there will be no loss of quality if an electronic copy of a sketch is required.

The use of layers when producing DTP layouts

Layers are a very useful feature of DTP software packages that help the user produce high-quality layouts. You may be asked to describe the advantages of using layers, some of which are described here. For example, layers can be:

- viewed together or separately – so they can be turned on or off to help edit particular parts of the layout
- used to create a master page for a multi-page layout
- reordered (moved backward or forward) to suit the layout at any time.

Layers also allow text and images to be edited separately – so individual layers can be edited with particular features that will not affect the other layers in the layout. Layers can also be locked to avoid them being edited by mistake.

Revision for your exam

A good revision technique is to work through as many SQA past papers as you possibly can. You can download these for free from the SQA website. Your teacher will also be able to provide you with older exam papers which may no longer be available on the SQA website. Use the marking instructions, which are also published on the SQA website, to check your work as you revise and to gain an understanding of areas you're struggling with.

You must set aside enough time for revision while still maintaining a healthy lifestyle. Exercise can help you relax and retain more information. You should take regular breaks from work to rest your brain. These breaks from revision are important because your brain needs time to embed new learning so that it can recall it more easily. Ensure you get plenty of sleep to give your brain a chance to turn new learning into long-term memories. This, in turn, makes new revision and learning easier, making your revision more efficient.

Good luck!

Revision Notes

You should use this space throughout the year to record any notes that will help you revise for your exam.

ISBN 9780008384425

Published by
Leckie
An imprint of HarperCollins Publishers
Westerhill Road, Bishopbriggs, Glasgow,
G64 2QT
T: 0844 576 8126 F: 0844 576 8131
leckiescotland@harpercollins.co.uk
www.leckiescotland.co.uk

Commissioning Editor: Sarah Mitchell
Project Manager: Fiona Watson

Special thanks to
Louise Robb (proofread)
Ken Vail (design and layout of first edition)
Jouve (typesetting of second edition)
Sarah Duxbury (cover design)

Printed and bound by CPI Group (UK) Ltd, Croydon CR0 4YY

A CIP Catalogue record for this book is available from the British Library.

Acknowledgements

P11 (br) © dboystudio / Shutterstock; P20 © NORBERT MILLAUER/DDP/AFP via Getty Images; P21 (bl) © Alexander Scharnweber / Alamy Stock Photo; P21 (br) © Alpha and Omega Collection / Alamy Stock Photo; P22 (tl) © Hugh Threlfall / Alamy Stock Photo; P22 (bl) © Shamleen / Shutterstock; P25 (bl) © Alexey Boldin / Shutterstock; P25 One Drive App © Daniel Krason / Shutterstock; P25 Dropbox App © iJeab / Shutterstock; P25 Google Drive App © Maxx Satori / Shutterstock; P29 (tr) © Diabluses / Shutterstock, Inc; P31 (bl) © Phanie / Alamy Stock Photo; P32 (t) © HarperCollins Publishers; P32 (b) Cultura Creative (RF) / Alamy Stock Photo; PP70-71 sketches © Scottish Qualifications Authority; P199 gym equipment models from www.grabcad.com

Sketches and drawings by Barry Forbes

All other images © Shutterstock.com

Whilst every effort has been made to trace the copyright holders, in cases where this has been unsuccessful, or if any have inadvertently been overlooked, the Publishers would gladly receive any information enabling them to rectify any error or omission at the first opportunity.